T0362956

PUBLISHED BY BOOM BOOKS

www. boombooks.biz

ABOUT THIS SERIES

....But after that, I realised that I knew very little about these parents of mine. They had been born about the start of the Twentieth Century, and they died in 1970 and 1980. For their last 20 years, I was old enough to speak with a bit of sense.

I could have talked to them a lot about their lives. I could have found out about the times they lived in. But I did not. I know almost nothing about them really. Their courtship? Working in the pits? The Lock-out in the Depression? Losing their second child? Being dusted as a miner? The shootings at Rothbury? My uncles killed in the War? Love on the dole? There were hundreds, thousands of questions that I would now like to ask them. But, alas, I can't. It's too late.

Thus, prompted by my guilt, I resolved to write these books. They describe happenings that affected people, real people. The whole series is, to coin a modern phrase, designed to push your buttons, to make you remember and wonder at things forgotten.

The books might just let nostalgia see the light of day, so that oldies and youngies will talk about the past and re-discover a heritage otherwise forgotten. Hopefully, they will spark discussions between generations, and foster the asking and answering of questions that should not remain unanswered.

BORN IN 1939?

WHAT ELSE HAPPENED?

RON WILLIAMS

AUSTRALIAN SOCIAL HISTORY

BOOK 1 IN A SERIES OF 33
FROM 1939 to 1971

War Babies Years (1939 to 1945): 7 Titles
Baby Boom Years (1946 to 1960): 15 Titles
Post Boom Years (1961 to 1971): 11 Titles

BOOM, BOOM BABY, BOOM

Published by Boom Books. Wickham, NSW, Australia

Web: www.boombooks.biz

Email: email@boombooks.biz

Third Printing 2021

© Ron Williams, December 2013

ISBN: 9780648324416

Creator: Williams, Ron, 1934- author.

Title: Born in 1939? : what else happened? / Ron Williams.

Edition: Soft back edition

Subjects: Nineteen forty-nine A.D.

  Almanacs, Australian.

  Australia--History--Miscellanea--20th century.

  Australia--Social conditions--20th century.

Cover Images. National Archives of Australia A1200, L11182A, Prime Minister Joseph Lyons; 1457/10, family outing; M3130, 75, rickshaw transport in Canberra; A1200, L21454, Dame Enid Lyons.

TABLE OF CONTENTS

IMPORTANT PEOPLE AND EVENTS

King of England	George VI
Prime Minister of Oz	Joseph Lyons
Leader of Opposition	John Curtin
Attorney General	Bob Menzies
The Pope	Pius XII
Prime Minister of Britain	Neville Chamberlain
US President	Franklin Roosevelt
Leader of Russia	Joseph Stalin
Emperor of Japan	Hirohito
Prime Minister of Japan	Hideki Tojo
Chancellor of Germany	Adolf Hitler

Winner of the Ashes:

1936-37	Australia 3 - 2
1938	Drawn 1 - 1
1946-47	Australia 3 - 0

Melbourne Cup Winners:

1938	Catalogue
1939	Rivette
1940	Old Rowley

Population of Australia   7 Million

INTRODUCTION TO THIS SERIES

I was five years old when the War started. But even at that early age, I was aware of the dread, and yet excitement, that such an epoch-making event brought to my small coal-mining town. At the start, it was not certain that it would affect us at all, but quickly it became obvious that everybody in the nation would be seriously involved in it. The most immediate response I remember was that all the Mums (who still remembered WWI) were worried that their sons and husbands would be taken away and killed. After that, I can remember radio speeches given by Chamberlain, Churchill, Lyons, Menzies, and Curtin telling of hard times ahead, but promising certain victory over our wicked foes.

For a young boy, as the War years went on, reality and fantasy went hand in hand. As I heard of our victories, I day-dreamed of being at the head of our Military forces, throwing grenades and leading bayonet charges. I sank dozens of battleships from my submarine that was always under attack. And I lost count of the squadrons of Messerschmitts that I sent spiraling from the sky. Needless to say, I was awarded a lot of medals and, as I got a bit older, earned the plaudits of quite a few pretty girls.

But, mixed in with all this romance were some more analytical thoughts. Every day, once the battles got going, I would go to the newspapers' maps of where the battlelines currently were. One for the Western front, one in North Africa, and a third in Russia. Later, another in the Pacific. Then I would examine them minutely to see just how far we had moved, backwards or forwards. I read all the reports, true and false, and gloated when it was said we were winning, and shrunk away from our losses.

At the personal level, I remember the excitement of getting up at 4am on a few days when nearby Newcastle was under submarine attack. We went to our underground air-raid shelter that we shared with a neighbour, and listened, and occasionally looked out, for some who-knows-what enemies to appear. It really was a bit scary. I can remember too the brown-outs, and the black-outs, the searchlights, the tank-traps, the clackers that were given to wardens to warn of gas attacks, and the gasmasks that 20 town-wardens (only) carried, presumably to save a town of 2,500 people when needed.

Then there was the rationing, the shortages of everything, and even the very short shirt tails that a perceptive Government decreed were necessary to win the cruel and needless War.

At the start of researching this book, everything began to come back to me. Things such as those above, and locations like Dunkirk, Tobruk, El Alamain, Stalingrad, and Normandy. Really, at this stage these names kept popping up, but I was at loss as to how significant they were. Also, names of people. Hitler and Mussolini I knew were baddies. But **how** bad? Chamberlain was always criticised for his appeasement, but what were his alternatives? Who **were** Ribbentrop and Molotov, and Tojo and Blamey, and what was Vichy France?

And finally, when war did come, and grind on, year after year, what effect did it have back here in Australia? How did we as a society cope with a world that just had to continue on, given that the sons and dads of the nation were actually being killed daily overseas? When the postman did his normal delivery and brought a letter saying your loved one is dead? What did we do when old jobs suddenly disappeared, and new ones were created a hundred miles away? When goods, long readily available, were no longer for sale? When everything changed?

It was all a hotch-potch to me when I started this series. At the end of it, I can say it is a lot clearer. I have sorted out the countable things like battles, locations, people, and rules and regulations. I can appreciate, too, the effects on society, though these can only be ascertained from what I **have** researched, and make no allowance for all the material that I have missed.

In presenting this book, I have started every chapter with a visit to Europe, and a look at the military events in the world, with increasing emphasis on the Pacific. Then I come back to Oz to see how we are faring in a military sense. After that, I blunder about reporting and speculating on which aspects of life here were affected by these, and other ongoing matters.

So, despite all the talk about the War above, and despite the fact that it was the controlling influence on all of our lives, the thrust of these books is about the **social changes and reactions that took place in this period, here in Oz.**

EUROPE'S LEGACY FROM EARLIER YEARS

Since the early 1920's, Hitler had seen his job prospects improve a lot. He had gone from being a political prisoner in jail to the undisputed leader of the German nation, with truly dictatorial powers that included the power of life and death over his subjects. By 1938, he was buttressed in his position by the all-pervasive and violent National Socialist Party (the Nazis), and also by the overwhelming support of most of the population.

One reason for his popularity was that he was the focal point of opposition to the vengeful Treaty of Versailles that ended WWI. Among other punishments, a multitude of German citizens was told they were no longer Germans (as national boundaries were added or changed), and that in fact they were now foreign nationals living in countries such as Austria, Czechoslovakia, and Poland. In 1938, these ex-pats had regained their national pride, and were stimulated by the violence and determination of the Nazis in Germany, and started to gather in organised gangs, and beat up the locals. These latter were only too pleased to reciprocate, so small regional patches of anarchy were becoming common, with deaths sometimes occurring as a consequence.

Hitler by then had circumvented Versailles restrictions on re-arming, and so had substantial military might. He had a dream of getting more Living Space (Lebensraum) for Germans, and decided that March, 1938, was the month to go for it. Over a period of only a couple of weeks, he bluffed and blustered and bullied the Austrians into giving up their national independence, and so **Austria was welcomed into the nation of Germany.** Six months later, the Sudetenland, about **half the area and population of Czechoslovakia, was returned to the fold** in a very similar manner.

Hitler, during the takeovers, had been clever enough to force the governments into asking for German help in suppressing the rioting that was occurring in their countries. So **he was then able to argue that the invading Germans were really peace-keepers**, but that he needed to install his own people and institutions so that they could do their job. Britain and France were tied by treaties to both the Austrians and Czechs, but they ignored these, and went along happily with the new status quo.

Chamberlain, Prime Minister of Britain, had been to Munich to sign off on this carve-up of Czech territory, and he and his umbrella were received back in England as a proper hero (by many) for having dispelled the war clouds that had been gathering. He brought with him a piece of paper, signed by Hitler, that promised that both of them would not deliberately make war on anyone. Now, as he famously said, we were guaranteed "peace in our times." In this book, we will look at just how right he was. **Perhaps you already know.**

AUSTRALIA'S LEGACY FROM EARLIER YEARS

In 1939 Australia, with a population soon to reach 7 million non-Aboriginal people, was plodding along as a happy member of the British Empire. Reasonably prosperous, it was quite content to be a few years behind the rest of the world in most things, and certainly wanted none of the madness that was currently affecting Europe.

Sadly, though, the state of semi-isolation could not last. Once again, as in WWI, we were certain to be dragged into that mad maelstrom. So, important people of all walks of life were now telling us that we needed to wake up to ourselves, and be ready to face tough times ahead. Our Prime Minister, Joseph Lyons, had just announced that he was **planning to re-introduce a militia (in effect, National Service) of 70,000 recruits over a few months**. And he announced the creation of Boards and groups of all sorts with bellicose intentions, and generally tried to prepare us for coming conflict.

Another outspoken harbinger of the oncoming doom was Lord Stanley Bruce, a former Prime Minister, and Australia's High Commissioner in London. Speaking at a Melbourne civic reception, he warned that:

War might come within a few months, a few weeks, or even a few days. If war came, Australia would certainly be involved. I would have liked to tell you of all that is being done to improve the world, that we are headed for an era of happiness and contentment, but all I can do is sound a grave and loud warning.

We will have to be a unified people with only one object. That is, to play our part without fear, and show that our attribute of displaying grit in the face of adversity is still with us, and that we are a virile people.

With messages such as this ringing in our ears, this peace-loving nation entered into the 1939 New Year, gradually conscious of the dangers ahead, but not at all keen to face up to them.

RULE BRITANNIA

There is no doubt that **Australians were completely loyal to Britain, and to the British Empire and the British**

Crown. There was no talk at all about republics, or about colonies seceding from the Empire, and no doubts about whether we should send troops to help Britain if a war broke out with Germany. It was just taken for granted that if this happened, **Australian troops would be sent straight** away, and that they would stay there until the war was over.

It could have been argued that, as a separate nation 12,000 miles from the conflict, we had no reason to send our men to be killed and maimed there. In fact, we could have taken the attitude that if we stayed out of the war, we could make a lot of money for our nation by sending supplies to the combatants. This was what American was planning and in fact did for the first two years. We could have done exactly the same.

But we did not. Quite the contrary. Despite the many bitter memories of the WWI that still filled the nightmares of a million Australians, this nation said from the beginning that we would go and fight again if the need arose.

Part of this loyalty came from the fact that most of the inhabitants of this fair land had come from Britain in the first place. And this meant that these persons themselves just took it for granted that the Empire would - must - rally to the flag. It was part of the Australian culture that every map of the world showed the Empire, always expanding so it seemed, in a pretty pink, and reminding everyone that it was the greatest Empire that the world had ever seen.

On top of that, there was a fervent loyalty to the Crown, and particularly to the Royal family. George VI, fairly new in the job, was winning hearts, and his pretty and vivacious wife Mary, and their two daughters, were winners as well.

In all, we as a nation were ready and willing to figuratively and literally pack up out troubles in the old kit-bag and smilingly offer our services to the Mother Country again.

EDUCATION, HEALTH, AND PENSIONS

I present below some brief material on these three matters. I will come back and talk about them later in this book, but a few introductory remarks, and comparisons with a period 70 years later, will help to set the scene.

Education. The average 20-year-old in 2019 has a High School education, and over half of them have a degree or some other ticket that suggests they might be worth employing. Eighty years earlier, about half of them had the Intermediate Certificate, and just a handful could boast any form of **Tertiary** education.

In fact, depending on where you were living, the majority of children left school as soon as they turned 14, and never went back to formal education. Large numbers of citizens could scarcely read, and fewer could write. This was especially true in the country, where ignorance of the world was compounded by great distances.

Many people could not read a **serious** argument in a newspaper, and some of these restricted themselves to the comics. Much more than half the population was able to boast that they had voted Liberal (or Labor) all their lives and had no intention of changing that. Almost no one born here had been overseas,yet large numbers of them were able to say with certainty that "Australia is the greatest country in the world". Legions were not at all conscious of anything resembling the arts or culture.

But this lack of education and liberal influences did not mean that half our fine citizens were yokels. Instead they were level-headed, sensible, industrious people with a great deal of common-sense who were living in an infant nation that would one day, soon, rise to a higher level of the finer things. With WWII out of the way, this aspiration was now starting to become a reality.

Health. Please don't ridicule me for stating the blindingly obvious. The nation's health **now** is vastly better that it was 80 years ago. We might all complain that doctors treat oldies like school children, and that the paper work at every level is almost crippling, and that the pills and tests take up all our free time. But we as a population are healthier than we ever were. **If you don't agree with me, ask your grannie. She died at the age of 65, while you will die at about 85.**

And its more affordable. Again we can complain about co-payments, and about doctors and specialists chiseling us, and about being sent for unnecessary tests that we have to cough out for. But it beats the situation in the past where frugal people had to forgo or delay treatment because they were broke or would be if they persisted.

Pensions. I will not talk much about these because I have a separate Section of this book discussing them. So, I will say that over the last 80 years, elderly people are much better off than they were. Again, you can talk about the faults in the current system and you are right to do so. But oldies in the main are better off now than ever before.

MY RULES IN WRITING

Note. Throughout this book, I rely a lot on re-producing Letters from the newspapers. Whenever I do this, I put the text in a different font, and indent it a little, and make the font somewhat smaller. **I do not edit the text at all.** That is, I do not correct spelling or grammar, and if the text gets at all garbled, I do not correct it. It's just as it was seen in the Papers.

Second note. The material for this book, when it comes from newspapers, is reported as it was seen at the time. If the benefit of hindsight over the years changes things, then I **might** record that in my **Comments**. The info reported thus reflects matters **as they were seen in 1939**.

Third note. Let me also apologise in advance to anyone I might offend. In a work such as this, it is certain some people will think I got some things wrong. I am sure that I did, but please remember, all of this is **only my opinion**. And really, **my opinion does not matter one little bit in the scheme of things. I hope you will say "silly old bugger", and shrug your shoulders and read on.**

Fourth note. Every Letter in this Book comes with a writer's name to make it easier for readers if they want to reference a particular Letter. I have **sometimes** included the address as well for **some British** Letters, because their **addresses are so novel to an Australian audience** that I could not ignore them. I offer them to you also, just for fun.

So, strap yourself in, and we will go out together and **win the coming War in a few easy months. It should be all over by Christmas.**

JANUARY: NEVILLE'S OUR MAN

Britain was a lot more relaxed in the New Year than it had been earlier during the Munich "crisis". Three months had passed and, while Hitler and Mussolini had continued on their provocative ways, nothing really worrying had emerged. At this time, it **was getting easier by the day to proclaim that Neville Chamberlain had indeed pulled off a masterpiece of diplomacy**, and that a lasting peace was now imminent.

This little eulogy from a *Times* Letter writer, all the way from Egypt, sums up the opinions of a host of people.

Letters, Abdul Nassar, Egypt. The other morning I received an official-looking Letter, from Egypt. It said *"Please accept my very warm thanks for your kind message. During these difficult and anxious times through which we have been passing the expressions of sympathy and good will which I have received from all quarters have been a source of great strength to me.*

Signed "Your very truly, Neville Chamberlain."

Frankly spoken, I was in ecstasy. Why not? I was in possession of the signature of the great Britisher who saved the world from disaster as a Minister for Peace. The Opposition may say what they like, the old man behaved with conscience, taking in consideration the welfare of humanity, of innocent children and mothers. I am sure that thousands of people who sent to him kind and encouraging messages have received such answers.

This act of courtesy is a proof of England's greatness and championship of democracy. To my short message of five simple words, *"Sincere congratulations, Champion of Peace,"* this was too much. As some men are born to disturb the peace of the universe in which we are condemned to live, there is one thing to rejoice and be consoled, that there are men, and not a few men, of conscience and character who are born peace-makers and conciliators.

Right now, at the start of the year, Britain was starting to fell good again, and millions from all over the nation were quite happy to rejoice that the great man had indeed brought them the peace that they all craved.

CIVIL DEFENCE

But still within Britain, all sorts of proposals were being made to help the nation's defence. Over the last few months, there had been suggestions that **trenches in backyards** might be adequate against air raids. These gave way to the proposal that the Government make available to each dwelling **a steel shelter that would be dug in underground**, or put in cellars. This was supposed to provide a bomb-proof capsule. **Now**, it was being proposed that **huge underground cavities be built under parks** and open spaces, and these be concreted to make them secure.

Letters, Thomas Bass, Reading. The thoughtful letter from Mr Geoffrey Faber on air defence in *The Times* of to-day, appears to me to be unanswerable. There are two policies and two policies only, open to us: either to evacuate large cities like London when air raids are imminent or to construct shelters that will render evacuation unnecessary.

Complete evacuation appears to me to be impossible. To remove even women and children is a task that would tax us to the uttermost. Furthermore, even if complete evacuation were possible it would be impracticable, as most of the normal activities of civilized life would then cease.

If then a large proportion of the adult population must remain in tempting targets like London, the only logical procedure is to provide the greatest possible protection for them, so that between raids they may be able to carry on.

In a recent number of the *British Medical Journal* I pointed out that our great London hospitals are defenceless, and that the medical profession cannot function adequately during enemy air raids if these hospitals are not provided with underground shelters. This at last has now been recognized, and a crusade is in progress to remedy the defect. But, if the civil population is not also protected, casualties will be so numerous that it will be physically impossible for the doctors to look after them all. We thus are driven to the inevitable conclusion that deep bomb-proof shelters to give 100 per cent protection is what we ought to provide at once. Such protection would give the essential moral support required by our people, and act as the greatest possible deterrent to those who build their hopes on winning a war by rapid knock-out attacks on the nerve centres of our normal activities – the great cities of England.

There were plenty of other perplexing worries.

Letters, Reverend Manton, Shipston on Stour.
Suppose you had dug trenches. It is easy to dig a
trench, but how is it to be kept free from water.
We who have churchyards in our care know how
quickly trenches flood. Constant pumping is
needed, and how is this to be provided?"

Letters, P Sisson, Newcastle-on-Tyne. Sandbags
and steel shelters are as much munitions of war
as guns and aeroplanes. Yet the Government is
making businesses pay for these. Would it make
them pay for searchlights, anti-aircraft guns and
fighter squadrons?

Letters, Alan Taylor, Dunchurch, near Rugby.
During the recent crisis many tons of sand were
imported into the large cities and towns for use in
filling sandbags. Sand by itself is about the most
useless material for this purpose, because a bag
filled with sand if hit by a bomb or shell direct
or by a splinter, bursts the bag and allows the
sand to run out. When this happens to the lower
layers in a wall, it is quite enough to cause the
collapse of the whole wall. Soil, quarry overburden
– preferably from a gravel quarry – or a material
containing clay should be used.

When filling the bag each shovelful of material
should be well bumped down to consolidate the
whole. If these bags are hit, less damage is done
by direct hit, and splinters bury themselves in the
bags. Further, bags so filled and built as a wall all
become settled. The fabric of the bag will rot away
leaving the contents intact, remaining so for many
months. Rotted bags, which were filled with sand,
just spill their contents.

Another writer had a different method of defence. He said that the best defence is attack.

Letters, Captain Chitty Thomas, Smeeth, near Asford, Kent. I am the head warden of a village situated a few miles from Lympne aerodrome; the London-Folkestone road passes through my sector. I can envisage circumstances when Lympne aerodrome would be fully engaged in defending itself. Then villages, scattered country houses, and traffic on the main road would be at the mercy of enemy aeroplanes flying low. These aeroplanes could select their targets at leisure and, flying slowly, could hardly fail to hit them. Any soldier will advise that the best defence is offence.

Accordingly, I would submit that selected villages should be supplied with a pom-pom gun (for technical reasons a pair would be very much better). There would be no difficulty in recruiting a couple of guns' crews from among the village wardens and utility squad men. They could be passed through a short artillery course, and there are ranges in the nearby for occasional practice.

The issue of these guns to a few villages would encourage recruiting both for A.R.P. and the other Services. It must be appreciated that A.R.P. work in the country calls for very different ideas from A.R.P. in towns.

Then, another approach was suggested by Mr Pierce, of Palmers Lane. He told us that "during the recent crisis, the conventional mask of artificiality was lifted, by fear and uncertainty, and men were driven to their knees because they knew that man alone could not prevail. Deliverances from immediate danger came from God. I would like to suggest that we might turn this time into days of national prayer, as deep and sincere as those days in September."

Finally, a good idea from Surrey. Mr Willson, of Haslemere, thinks that the warbling warning of air raids is a depressing one, and wants to change it. Perhaps the inspiring "**prepare to receive cavalry**" would do. Also, a second one might be "**the charge**". We would all then be a lot safer, surely.

EVACUATION FROM LONDON

Another proposal that was attracting much attention was that, if and when London and other major cities were bombed, **all children should be evacuated** from their city homes, and moved to places in the country likely to be free from attack. Obviously there are many difficulties in the administration of such a scheme.

Letters, Latymer, Shipton-onychwood, Oxford.

Is it advisable to move children from parts of London – e.g. Hampstead and Highgate – which are not likely to be subjected to intensive attack and plant them in villages situated close to one of the many Air Force aerodromes in the Home Counties? These aerodromes are, one imagines, quite certain to be attacked if war comes, and any village within a couple of miles is likely to suffer. Yet, to my own knowledge, several such villages received parties of London children in the September crisis. One could not help thinking that they were being moved from the frying-pan to the fire.

There were also problems with staffing. Many **middle-class Britishers had live-in maids**, many of whom were ready to change jobs at minimum provocation. The pressing question was **how would these young ladies react to households being filled with numbers of sundry and unruly children.**

Letters, Mrs Wade, Oxford. Householders, shortly to be approached under the refugee billeting scheme, await enlightenment on several points. For example, what authority will they be given over the conduct of their augmented households; and/ or is any system for the inspection or discipline of the evacuated population in billets contemplated? Further, many houses to which refugees may be allocated cannot be run single-handed owing to their size.

Will the domestic labour which makes the present working of these larger houses possible – labour already to say the least of it, fluid – be available when the emergency arises, or will it be free to take flight at the approach of the refugees, leaving the housewife to cope unaided with the immigration? It is perfectly clear that pressure in one form or another will be used on the mistress of the house in this matter. If so, could not pressure be brought to bear on the maid also?

Barry Curtis from Nottingham pointed that out he was a quite elderly bachelor, living alone in a large house. He did not feel happy with the letter he recently received that said "please hold yourself in readiness to receive … at any time of the day or night….20 children." He pointed out that 20 German soldiers might be acceptable, but he had doubts about 20 children.

Letters, Dorothy Gordon, Manchester City. I wonder whether the aged or incapacitated could also be migrated to the country. I see a lot of similarities with children, and thought it would save the nation money if attacks were to happen.

OTHER DEFENCE ISSUES

Propaganda was being increasingly used by both the British and the Germans against each other. Both parties in 1939 were making broadcasts, in both languages, to the other, and were laying it on thick. The British were, of course, more reserved and were inclined to talk about the sublimeness of life in a democracy. The German broadcasts were less subtle, and were full of accounts of British atrocities, and of the weaknesses in its armed forces and defences.

Letters, Ralph Savory, Knockbtreda, Belfast. The German anti-British propaganda is again being broadcast from all their wireless stations, and on the evenings of January 2 and 3 exceeded all bounds. At 9 o'clock, from Hamburg a statement was broadcast in which the British troops in Palestine were accused of "monstrous cruelties" There is no way that British troops would behave in that way. The whole diatribe was an insult to the British culture, and the way parents raise their children. We are a honourable race, and such barbarities are unknown to us.

The British Government has great technical resources at its disposal, and it is surely not too much to ask that these effusions should be carefully recorded with a view to an official protest.

He might have felt a little better if he had realised the Brits were reciprocating, though in a more subdued manner.

Then of course there were the current loopholes in the new provisions for **reserved occupations**. These were the jobs that were considered necessary for producing essential services and goods, so the persons working in them were not allowed to leave to join the Services. In Britain, they included accountants and other professions. Later, in Australia they would include coalminers, wharf labourers and steel workers. Mr Underwood, of Cavendish Square, was **a solicitor** and thought that he should well be protected from serving. "In a war affecting the civilian population, the duties of an executor and trustee would become even more difficult, necessary, and numerous. It seems that the omission of solicitors from the list of reserved occupations is an oversight that should and can be easily rectified."

MEANWHILE, BACK IN OZ

Joseph Lyons, our Prime Minister, had been in the job for years. The newspapers were getting all excited because by April 22 he would have been in office for seven years, three months, and 22 days. That is, longer than any previous occupant, and they thought we needed to be reminded of this daily.

Over the last few months he had been pushing the idea that Australia must prepare for a military crisis, and in particular he had led the Government to re-introduce the creation of a militia, of 70,000 men. Rightly or wrongly, so it seemed at the time, he had apparently hitched his political bandwagon to preparations for war, and throughout January he kept grinding away at that these. On January 26, he made a statement after a meeting of the Defence Council. In it, he said "I am forced to believe that some of our people have not grasped the significance of our situation. Some seem content to move in a world which belongs to yesterday, **or else are blind to blunt facts**."

People across the nation were outraged, and stirred into correspondence. Letters poured into the newspapers complaining that Lyons would claim that it was **the people** who were not aware of the true situation. Writer after writer claimed that it was **Lyons who was out of touch.** A day after his speech, **the Melbourne** *Argus* **published seven letters under the heading "Who is blind?"**, and to avoid repetition I have made a single composite Letter from them

MELBOURNE *ARGUS***.** Thirty years ago, before Japan attained her present strength, and was then a friendly power, and before the rise of the dictator States, Lord Kitchener recommended a trained force of **300,000** to defend Australia.

Contrast the present state of affairs and ponder on the opinion of the Government and present military advisers who say **70,000** is adequate. Despite Mr Lyons's eloquence in pointing out the dangers we are facing, he seems to be completely fixed on this 70,000. But nothing short of the whole resources of the Commonwealth will suffice. What we need is **universal** military training for all suitable men, with no exceptions. If Mr Lyons is right, we need our men trained right now, and his idea of a military force that has a camp once a year is out of the question. There is no doubt that, despite the service he has done for this nation, he is past it, and should give way to a younger man made of sterner stuff.

But we should return to the claim that we are asleep and blind to serious facts. What are these facts? He gives us speeches full of time-worn platitudes about some dangers, but what **are** the facts? Why does he refuse to take us into his confidence? By withholding these facts, he is acting like the very dictators whose methods we have no time for.

Then suppose we accept the 70,000. It is likely that only one-tenth of that number will be available for fighting in the front line. Wake up. That is not a significant number. Further, it is not only the men that we short of, but also horses. There is nothing more mobile than mounted men, and **no mechanised troops could carry out raids such as we saw in the last war**.

There is also the need for other Services, not just the Army. We have neither the time nor the money to build an expensive navy, but we could have a big Air Force. The recruitment for this should start immediately, and the manufacture of flying and fighting machines should become top priority

In short, we need a Government who faces up to the whole situation, and simply harping on one aspect of it for political gain is a sham.

Letters flooded in to all the major city papers. They showed that Lyons apparently had no understanding of the Australian public on this topic. He had opened a can of worms and, as worms do, they were standing up and hissing at him. The deluge did not stop.

Letters, W Hoddinott, Nagambel. Would it be possible to enlist a unit that does not deal with horses? Would it not be possible to accommodate these in a **cycle** battalion? The average young man is usually able to ride a bike, and there would be no difficulty in getting sufficient numbers **who would bring their own machines**.

Letters, Marshall Lyle. Our oil depots are concentrated in a few very small areas, and that they need to be dispersed throughout the country. Our great space of territory and our covering bush are in our favour. The bush would aid guerrilla defence in the country districts, where **the enemy planes would get lost**.

Letters, Sir Norman Brooks, President of the Lawn Tennis Association of Australia. There are no men more suitable for the adequate defence of Australia than our sportsmen, and I have not the slightest doubt that when they realise the necessity for preparedness, the necessary man-power will be readily available.

Letters, Ex-Digger. Once again Joseph Lyons has issued a grave warning about the crisis that may develop at any moment, and his claim that the people are only lukewarm toward his warnings. Perhaps the boot is on the other foot, as they realise only too well the position, but as they put him and his party into power, it is for him to give us a lead. Why does not he bring in compulsory training – he has the power, and not waste any more time with **the voluntary system, which will never be a success**, as it is only the loyal men who are helping to keep it alive. To a returned soldier of four and a half years' service, I know the dangers of putting untrained men up against fully trained men, so let us prepare properly now, before the crisis arrives. **Let us have action!**

H G WELLS IN AUSTRALIA

Herbert George Wells was a well-known English writer. In 1939, he was famous for being the "creator of the science fiction" genre, and for his heartfelt **writings on socialism**. He was now in Australia because **his early training in the physical sciences** had entitled him to speak at a learned science symposium being held in Canberra. While he was in this country, he attracted much public attention, and gave dozens of talks and press interviews.

In these very forthright encounters he expressed his disrespect and antagonism towards the Fascist waves that were affecting Europe, and **his dislike for the dictators**, Hitler, Mussolini and the new Spanish dictator, Franco. His were pretty common-place sentiments at the time, and were in no way remarkable. Mr Lyons thought differently.

It is to be regretted, however, that while in Australia, Mr Wells has so far indulged his well-known political sympathies so as to make disparaging remarks **about the leaders of other nations**.

It happens that the nations whose leaders are the subjects of the wit of Mr Wells have systems of government which differ from our own.

While different systems of Government may offer the occasion for differences of opinion, serious argument, deep conviction, and even clever phrase-making, I consider that **personal insults offered**

to the leaders of one nation by the citizens of another nation are to be deplored.

As British people, we would not appreciate foreigners offering insults to members of the Royal Family, or to any other of our national leaders, even if these remarks were made by persons as widely known as is Mr Wells in his own country.

I would prefer that Mr Wells should exercise his undoubted gifts for the promotion of **international understanding rather than otherwise.**

For the second time in a month, Mr Lyons found himself in the hot seat. **Once again, commentary and Letters railed against him.** He was criticised for trying to restrict free speech, in that Wells was simply expressing his own opinion. And also for giving tacit support to the regimes under Wells' attack. Lyons later explained that his aim was to make it clear that the views expressed by Wells were not the official views of the Australian Government, and pointed out that Australians would not like it if an outsider criticised the Queen. The replies to **that** statement were quite forthright. **Firstly**, no one even thought for a moment that Wells was speaking for anyone but himself. **Secondly**, as a correspondent wrote, "the Queen is not a malevolent dictator, but the other three blokes are."

Comment. Lyons did himself no good during these scraps. He gave the impression of losing his way, and of being under great pressure.

BOOTS ARE NOT MADE FOR WALKING

Letters, Mary Prior. The scooter is losing popularity, partly because it is generally regarded as a nuisance in the streets, but chiefly because of its devastating effect on shoes.

Mothers have discovered that the one-leg action demanded by the scooter resulted in the rapid wearing out of one shoe of each pair, and shoe repairers found that single shoes, instead of pairs, were being brought to them for resoling. At the height of the scooter popularity it was quite seriously suggested that manufacturers might meet the situation by supplying children's street shoes in threes instead of in pairs.

The really grave harm that can be caused by the frequent use of a scooter was emphasised by a recent case. In this case a child, who had developed unsteadiness, and was apparently unable to stand, was thought by its parents to be suffering from infantile paralysis. Careful observation by the doctor led him to a different conclusion, and his final verdict was that the really serious condition of the small boy had been brought about by the persistent use of his scooter, which had induced a lack of muscular balance.

The provision of suitable shoes for children is not a simple problem. Bunions, for example, are as a rule the result of wearing shoes too short for the foot at some stage in the early growing period. The big toe, unable to find room ahead, leans over to one side in order to avoid the pressure, and gradually the joint at its base is forced outwards, and the resulting pressure on the joint sets up a bunion. The practice of allowing children to go barefoot whenever possible, and the fashion of wearing sandals, have made distorted feet much less common than they were 10 or 15 years ago. But the problem, of how to provide for children shoes made of good leather or other suitable material at a reasonable price, still remains to be solved. In the winter time leather shoes are a necessity.

SWAGMEN

News item. At the Tumut Police Court, John James Quinton, aged 30 years, swagman, was fined 30 Pounds, in default 60 days imprisonment, for having left a fire in the open air which he had not thoroughly put out.

Evidence was that he had lit a fire in a stump in the Church of England grounds at Brungle to boil his billy. The Chairman of the Bench commented on the practice of leaving un-attended fires in this hot weather.

Comment. Thirty Pounds, in those days, was a small fortune. Quinton elected to serve the 60 days.

BANJO PATTERSON

News item, January 2. Andrew Barton Patterson, Writer, was awarded a CBE in the King's New Year's Honours List. The official citation read "Andrew Barton Patterson is a solicitor of the Supreme Court of NSW. He was a correspondent at the South African War, the Spanish American War, and was in China at the end of the Boxer Rebellion and at the beginning of the Great War. He is a well-known Australian poet."

FEBRUARY: BBC UNDER ATTACK

The British Broadcasting Corporation was owned by the Government, but was supposedly an independent body that was charged with providing conservative and factual News Services for the benefit of the British public. At this time, a number of critics of the Service claimed that, in reporting European news, it was exaggerating the bad news from the dictatorships so that, as always happens in worrying times, the population would rally to the incumbent government.

Letters, Baker White. Surely the news broadcast at 9pm on the National wavelength yesterday was a striking example of what seems to be a deliberate attempt by the BBC to scare the listeners out of their lives before they go to bed. The bulletin contained the following items of "news," arranged, if my memory serves me right, in the following order:

One. Signor Mussolini is to make an important speech at Turin. **Two.** Units of the Italian fleet now in South American waters are being hastily recalled. **Three.** Herr Lutze, the head of the German Storm Troopers, has cancelled his visit to Libya and is returning immediately to Berlin.

Four. Germany will have mobilized over 1,000,000 men by March 1.

As a matter of curiosity, I listened in to the 10 o'clock London Regional bulletin on the same evening, to find that items 1, 3 and 4 had disappeared from the news, presumably because the BBC had discovered, very tardily, that there was no truth in the mobilization rumour, and that the story about

Herr Lutze was 90 per cent fiction and 10 per cent fact. Further comment seems to be superfluous.

Letters, Michael Hartley. I am afraid the BBC cannot altogether be blamed for reporting general tidings of woe, whether Imperial or foreign, because they are, only too evidently, what the public wants. Calamity, especially when it affects women, is always news: we never tire of hearing about girls trapped in burning buildings. But in their summaries of current events in totalitarian States they do, I think, select those items which are most likely to grate on a democratic ear.

I was in Rome at the end of November, and found English people there who were anxious for a better understanding between ourselves and Italy much distressed by the tendentious nature of BBC reports. Their account of Count Ciano's speech, I was told, while doing full justice to its disturbing passages, omitted any reference to the loud and prolonged cheers which greeted the names of Lord Perth, Mr Chamberlain, and Lord Halifax.

However, I object to the one-sided nature of the news. Every item that tends to place the Fascist nations in an unfavourable light is collected by the BBC and emphasised for the benefit of millions of viewers. **I fear our policy of appeasement is considerably hindered by our news bulletins, and that international hatred and ill will is generated by them.**

Night after night, we are presented with lurid extracts from Continental newspapers that, on the following morning, are found to be worthy of a few lines in subsidiary pages of responsible papers.

Mr Berry, of Roade Vicarage, went all grammatical on us. He argued that "We might have been told that Mr X had been recalled by Herr Hitler; instead we are told he was "hurriedly" recalled. The adverb adds nothing to the meaning of the word "recall"; but it does convey suggestions of menace and crisis that some of your correspondents have been deploring. We could do with fewer adverbs and adjectives in the news."

Perhaps, it was suggested, the BBC could learn something from overseas.

Letters, H Abrahamson. Dutch stations broadcast plain statements of fact (so far as I am aware never a rumour) without stressing either the spoken word or the relative value of items. The voice is not dropped to a mournful dirge when some eminent personage dies, nor does youthful ecstasy allow itself free rein if it rejoices at the arrival at Croydon of a long-distance flyer, or what not.

In a quiet monotone the Dutch news announcers relate the main items of news of the day without either salt, sugar, or paprika added. Clearly these announcers are men of mature years whose personal emotions are quite subsidiary to the simple task entrusted to them.

Letters, Ronald Leslie-Melville, Monte Carlo. I think the BBC might well imitate the French technique of news presentation, which is personal instead of being impersonal. This is the factor that makes all the difference, no matter what the news itself may be. A French news bulletin, whether from a State or a private station, is heralded by the announcement: "Here is Monsieur Quelquechose to give you the latest news." Monsieur Quelquechose then tells us the news, but does not **announce** it. To the listener he is not a *deus ex machina*, but an ordinary human being who has read all the dispatches from the news agencies. He links the items of news together, reminds us briefly of the background to the events he has to describe, and, if necessary, tells us not to pay too much attention to one item or another as its news-value is still doubtful. In short, although the bulletin is usually supplied by Havas, the French equivalent of Reuters, it is presented to the listener for what it is worth.

Letters, Ronald Jeans, London. The news selector of the BBC should not be a man schooled in the journalistic arts of Fleet Street, because his skill is wasted on a medium which needs completely different arts. We can choose what we read in our newspapers, but not to what we listen in our news bulletins on the wireless.

All disquieting rumour should be ignored until fact is to hand. The absence of rumour-reports in *The Times* is one of the great attributes of your paper and the cause of many of us saying, "Let's see what *The Times* says," in moments of crisis.

Surely the BBC, with its power to stiffen the nation's morale, **should keep the news as cheerful as possible**, leaving the sensational morning papers to scare us, when we are fresh from sleep and in a better state to assess the truth of the reports?

The BBC leapt to its own defence. It could scarcely comment on matters of taste, it said, because opinions differed from person to person. **When people were upset they were more inclined to write strong Letters**, while satisfied persons did not.

But it could comment on fact. It was able to, triumphantly, point out that two factual opinions criticising it, were indeed wrong. **The first** said that, in its early bulletins each night, it would spend a certain amount of time on an item, but that in its later Bulletin it would have either pulled it altogether, or had it cut down to half, because it had found out that it was faulty. The Corporation said the only reason for this was that the second Bulletin was only half as long as the first, and some things had to go.

The second charge against them was even easier to defeat. The critic quoted a German newspaper, *Das Schwarze Korps*, as a constant source of criticism of Britain from within Germany, and **said the BBC always quoted it**. It turned out that only once **this year** (that is, January) had the BBC quoted from this source, and on that occasion the newspaper had been indeed complimentary to Britain. (Note that **all of last year** had been a different story). So, sadly against the true state of play, the BBC won **opportunistically** on this point also.

Support for the BBC came also from two Parliamentarians. One of them, an ex-journalist, pointed out that the BBC took its news from a limited number of wire services, such as Reuters. The only reason an item got on to the News was that it had some **sauce** to it, and there was no market for homilies and platitudes. So the BBC each night had the choice between "Source One sauce and Source Two sauce."

He knew that it generally opted for the more moderate one, but it did have to report something on developing matters.

The second Parliamentarian looked at the business aspect of broadcasting. All radio stations were competing for listeners, and the BBC had to include a certain amount of spice (rather than sauce) if it wanted to get its market share. In fact, **the BBC was torn** between those inside it who wanted to sensationalise the news more, and those who wanted to adopt a straight reporting of known facts, like *The Times* tended to do. The News Bulletins now delivered were the result of the ongoing compromises reached.

Evelyn Waugh, the renowned writer, chimed in with a comment from a different world.

May I commend to your readers who find themselves painfully excited by the BBC news an economical and unfailing solution? We are fortunate enough to live in a country where listening-in is not yet compulsory. I have no wireless machine and find my morning newspaper a perfectly adequate source of information. Is this very odd?

Mr Bell, of Leeds saw the situation differently. He conceded "that everyone has his own approach to listening. But someone who is so cut off from the momentous events of the day, as to have no radio, is in no position to advise other people on what they should listen to or behave. Further, if I pay radio licence fees to the BBC, I expect them, first and foremost, to provide a reliable News Service, and not just say I don't want it by turning it off."

The last word here goes to Mr Crompton below.

Letters, R Crompton, Ramsbottom, Manchester.
God help this country if those correspondents who
nightly go to bed shaking with fright after they
have heard the BBC news are typical citizens. I
find the bulletins very stimulating and an effective
antidote to the lethargy induced by the emasculated
headlines and news in *The Times*.

A FEW MORE MILITARY MATTERS

**Opinion on winning wars. Letters, Commander
Geoffrey Bowles, Catherine Place.** Modern War
is a matter of cargoes.   The side that gets the
cargoes wins the war. If both sides get cargoes, the
war will be long.   England can win wars without
armies and by sea power alone by taking enemy
cargoes and convoying ours.

My oath. News Item. When the King and Queen go to
Newcastle for the launching of the new battleship King
George V on February 21, schoolchildren will be required
to take an oath of allegiance to his Majesty.

It will read "I do swear by Almighty God that I will be
faithful and bear true allegiance to his Majesty King George
VI, his heirs and successors, according to the Law, so help
me God."

Air raid shelters. Letters, Major H Browning. It
is simply a tragedy to see our parks and gardens
being turned into air raid shelters, when it is clear
that 90 per cent of them will never be made use
of.   For instance, I live within a stone's throw of
Eaton Square, the gardens of which are now being
dug up. Now, every single house in Eaton Square
has its own ready-made shelter in the shape of

cellars, basements and areas; these with a little instruction could be made splinter, shock, and gas proof inside half an hour, and residents in Eaton Square would not be such fools as to leave these shelters and run over to dug-outs in the gardens, which cannot afford one-tenth of the protection given in the home.

Let there be light. Auguste Busshe, Chancery Lane. There are numerous reports of a large demand for candles since the scare of last autumn. As a London antique dealer, I can also report there has been a very substantial increase in interest in candlesticks, especially those made of brass or copper. Can it be that the fear of war has brought back to our rooms an appreciation of the traditional softness of candlelight and the beauty of metal work?

BACK IN AUSTRALIA

Joseph Lyons, Prime Minister, was in a difficult situation. Things had moved too fast for him, or anyone, since he brought down the Federal Budget last August. After the crisis in September, he had realised that the world was just one mistake away for a near-disaster, and so he then responded with his call for the 70,000 militia.

Clearly, by now, the nation thought he had not done enough. His problem was that any additional moves on his part involved big expenditure, and he was stuck with the current year's budget. **He could hardly say this**, because the Opposition would crucify him for getting his budgeting wrong. So, he had to make do until the next budget.

In February, he made a few rather successful attempts to do this. **Firstly**, he announced that a new permanent military force of 10,000 men would be formed as a mobile unit ready to act anywhere required. But the caveat was that it would need "provision for equipment, barracks, uniforms, training, and personnel." So that the unit would be set up sometime in the future, and might take a few years to reach its full head count. Not much cost involved here.

This was a pretty weak gesture, but it was significant because it showed for the first time the Lyons was aware that his 70,000 men were not adequate.

Secondly, he gleefully told the nation that production of ammunition and small arms had doubled since last September. The number of workers at Lithgow and other small arms factories had doubled, and they were about to expand further into a second shift. Things were happening, it appeared.

Thirdly, he announced, again, that his Commonwealth War Book would soon be released. This would be a compilation of various plans that the Public Service had produced, **detailing plans for action in the event of war**.

For example, what would happen to food resources and distribution? If men left the land in droves, where would the food come from? If petrol got really scarce, how would the food be moved from place to place? Should food be stored in large depots, or in small de-centralised depots? There was no doubt that certain industries had to keep producing at their current levels. Could the current workers be allowed to enlist? What powers did the Commonwealth have to intervene here? And what powers did it have to introduce rationing?

These, and thousands of other questions, were to be answered by a dozen Committees, and published in the War Book. When he announced some months earlier that it was to be prepared, it was seen to be a good move, and now that it was almost completed, the public also duly noted it. But, for Mr Lyons, appreciation of it was too often forgotten in society's fixation on things military.

Comment. It is very easy, with hindsight, to applaud these measures. But remember, **Lyons did not have hindsight as an aid to policy making**. He must have always been conscious of the possibility that **peace could suddenly break out**, and that ridicule would fall on him from all sides for scare-mongering.

Public opinion. So, at the end of February, commentary was still voluminous and resolutely critical of Lyons' voluntary recruitment scheme. I won't dwell on this again here, and will just add a few Letters, some of them sensible.

Letters, A Jenkin. Let the Government purchase half a million of the finest modern rifles at once. Distribute them at depots throughout the Commonwealth, with plenty of ammunition, and make it compulsory for every able-bodied man in the land to attend long-range rifle practice every Saturday afternoon. In 12 months we would at least have half a million men (all ages) who know how to use a gun even if we haven't an army. **Give me a gun and a hole in the ground, and I'll guarantee to do my share.**

Letters, P Tooles. Would it not be possible for our Government to absorb **the unemployed** according to their various capacities on regular defence duties and training? Would it not form a standard and efficient army corps, and at the same time, help these men to maintain their sense of usefulness? Supposing that it did cost the Government a slight increase on present sustenance costs, what added prestige to Australia, what added strength for defence purposes, and what added self-respect to the unfortunate "susso"! Above all, what a solution to the unemployment problem. Why not let men be men and carry out their right to live and work for their country and their own?

Letters, K Kraft. I think I am right in saying that all the people of Australia and of the Empire are unanimous in their desire for peace. The question is, how is peace to be attained? On this point we are not unanimous. Some put their trust in rearmament, others in a change of the present economic system, others, again, in what is termed "following the Prince of Peace." In pressing our own particular point of view, are we not in danger of defeating the end desired by all? There is a common basis on which all Christians, at any rate, can take their stand, and **that is prayer**.

During the crisis there was formed in London an organization known as "The League of Prayer and Service." Millions in all parts of the world have joined the League. I have been asked by the promoters to do what I can to let the objects of the League be known here in Australia. I should be glad to send particulars to any who might be interested.

Letters, Aussie, Koromburra. I have been asked by men on the track (swagmen) what they have to fight for if war should occur. My answer to them (because they noticed my Gallipoli badge) has been to take a walk to any school and watch the children coming out and they would get the answer. I have reminded them that these children are of the same national blood as themselves, and that even the little ant, fighting and struggling for its food every day, would still fight to the death for its own.

I cannot understand the apathy of our people. We asked in 1914 for volunteers and got 400,000 or somewhere near it, to offer to go overseas to a foreign country to fight. Yet when the call comes for volunteers to fight for their own country, instead of half a million volunteering, it is just hard work to gather 70,000. What of the motto, Advance Australia? Why the blood streams of Australians should have slowed down, below the heat of the old Anzac spirit, is more than I can comprehend after their glorious war-time record. Personally, I am out of work, but I still would march behind the band playing "Advance Australia Fair."

Letters, T Adeney, Elwood. Some silly people are saying "Give back to Germany the colonies that were filched from her after WWII. It is she who owns them." "Filched" indeed! It is carrying the policy of appeasement to ridiculous extremes to repeat such piffle. The colonies really belong not to Germany but to the natives of the countries concerned, from whom they were filched by the now rapacious Germany.

ADVICE FOR SMART WOMEN

A French fashion expert, known only as Mademoiselle, was visiting **the largest** Melbourne retail store and giving tips on the latest happenings in the fashion capital of the world, Paris. *The Argus* approached her for her advice and she obliged with the following dictums.

Few women have beautiful knees, so – we hide them. She pointed to the new short skirts she had brought to Melbourne with her. "You think the girls here won't wear them. But they will", she predicted. It was necessary to have **the short skirts just below the knees**, and the wearer must have shapely legs. To get these, she said, a little emphasis must be placed on exercises, and the appearance of the legs will thus be improved far more than by having beautiful stockings worn with the seam in correct position. Strangely, she said, seams had an odd way of sliding to the left or the right on some legs, and they should be adjusted carefully and frequently.

Her wisdom did not stop there. "Many young women allow themselves to walk in a slovenly way, and this produces the first symptoms of knock-knees and weaknesses of the muscles. This can be overcome by walking in the correct manner below.

"First of all there is the position of readiness: the arms should swing naturally from the shoulders, the right arm swinging forward with the left leg, and the left arm with the right leg.

The legs must have a natural and free movement from the hips. The knees must be kept straight, except while the leg is being carried forward, when the knee must bend slightly to enable the foot to clear the ground.

The foot must be carried straight to the front and placed on the ground by an easy and free movement."

AN APPLE A DAY

Letters, Walter Edwards. While no Britisher can approve of the totalitarian system of government, we can learn a few things from these progressive countries. Consider, for example, the growing use of pure fruit in Germany. According to an Australian woman who has recently been abroad, "the beer and sausage has gone, the fruit has come, and the "corporation' has gone." Visitors to America tell the same story. The increased consumption of pure fruit juices in Australia would build up the health of the nation, and rejuvenate and extend our declining fruit-growing industry.

INSPECTION OF MOTOR VEHICLES

Various authorities were making suggestions that motor vehicles should be examined prior to the renewal of their registration. This followed reports that many old vehicles were on the road and that safety issues were becoming apparent as these the average age of vehicles rose.

Not everyone could see the wisdom of this.

Letters, H Harrison, Secretary, Chamber of Auto Industries. Your editorial in Monday's issue, **criticising the proposal for the compulsory examination of motor vehicles**, has the complete support of this chamber. We have been investigating similar legislation in other places, and find that it has no beneficial effect, but rather the reverse. **It creates additional work for the police, is a further tax on road-users, and is an irritation with negative results.**

In Victoria the motorist has **to present his vehicle to the police** before he obtains his renewal registration disc. In New South Wales, the police post to the motorist his new registration papers, and therefore the police never see the vehicle at time of renewal. It is estimated in New South Wales that such legislation would cost motorists 120,000 pounds a year. In New Zealand the value, as well as the reliability of the certificates, have been questioned by judges.

The frequent criticism of old vehicles is not justified by actual results in relation to accidents. Figures prove that accidents are less frequent with old vehicles than with new vehicles. This chamber is satisfied that nothing would be gained by compulsory examination of motor vehicles, and thoroughly supports *The Argus* viewpoint.

RIFLE CLUBS AS A WAR LOOMS

There had been a lot of interest lately in having ordinary citizens trained in the handling of weapons. Such Letters as the one below sought to answer a list of questions about the rather mysterious workings and philosophies of rifle clubs.

Letters, R Dimmick, Hon Secretary, Legion of Frontiersmen Rifle Club, Montmorency. "Rifleman's" letter conveys rather too gloomy a picture. But I agree with him that it seems peculiar to limit membership of rifle clubs at this time. If, however, there are any men who would like to join a club shooting on the Williamstown range, we have a few vacancies in ours. Several of our members have joined the militia.

Membership need not be expensive. Club subscription is 10/- per annum. We have some club-owned rifles suitable for beginners, but a rifle can be purchased through the club from the Defence Department for one pound deposit and one pound per year for four years. Ammunition is granted to "efficient" members free. To be classed "efficient" a minimum of three shoots a year are necessary. Railway travel from Melbourne to Williamstown is by free pass. The only other expense is one shilling each, which we pay the marker.

A RARE VOICE FROM INDIA

Letters, P Pocha, Poona. Melbourne. Allow me to introduce myself as an Indian, going through your country on a short holiday trip. I have read in *The Argus* Week-end Magazine a very interesting article, "Who and What is the Grand Mufti?" Without reference to the rest of the article, I wish to take exception to one remark, the significance of which creates prejudice and misunderstanding between people dividing this small earth into two distinct parts, East-West; good-bad. In discussing "awful acts of terrorism," the writer speaks of people of the East thus: "They do not share our Western horror of them, but then, East is East and West is West."

Will you please tell me where and how you divide the globe between East and West? If geographically, where does Australia come in? Or do you mean European and Asiatic? If so, will you please tell me where you put the idol of your living life, the Apostle of love and truth – Jesus Christ – East or West, and what do you know of the most modern and living example of the same love and truth – Mahatma Gandhi – is he East or West?

What about the atrocity stories that your own papers printed in 1914 about the Germans – are the Germans East or West, and what about the present many German concentration camps and their Jews? Which of the two is better, the Grand Mufti or Hitler and his followers East or West?

We remember the massacres of helpless Indians at Amritsar. Was General Dyer East or West?

I, an Easterner, lay no claim to any superiority over you Westerners; in one sphere of life or the other we are all made of the same clay, cast in the same mould, some baked more, some less. We all have the same passions, same love, same hate, some more and some less. Let us not, in this lovely land, in this young country of yours, create ugly boundary lines, create ugly thoughts of East or West, North or South.

Comment. This plea in this Letter to avoid thoughts of East versus West was an early harbinger of developments after the War. Right now, in 1939, the average Australian knew that the white man (and woman) was superior, and that the white man had the right to rule, **right round the**

world, and that coloured people were lucky to enjoy the benefits that the white man always brought with him.

By the time the War was over, all coloured peoples had a very different view of these truths, and were ready to fight, for half a century, against them.

ADVICE FROM *WORLD OF WOMEN*

In case you have been wondering, the above popular magazine ruled on a few matters.

It would not be correct for a bridegroom to wear a dinner suit at a wedding to take place at 2.50 pm, even though the bride plans to wear conventional bridal wear. He should wear full morning dress or a navy blue suit, with grey tie and white shirt and collar.

Would it be correct for the matron to wear a long lace frock or whether a black tailored costume would be more suitable?

If the wedding is very formal, the long dress could be worn, but if it is to be informal and the bridegroom is wearing an ordinary suit, the costume would be more suitable for the occasion, assuming that "matron" means the bride's mother or bridegroom's mother.

How to clean and stiffen a white panama school hat?

Panama hats may be cleaned without injury to the straw. A strong solution of borax with warm water is suitable for the purpose. Apply this with a small scrubbing brush, and when the hat is thoroughly clean, rinse it in a bowl of warm water and put in the open air to dry. It is best laid on a flat surface, with weights on the brim and a basin inside the crown. This will keep it in good shape, and will also prevent it from shrinking.

Home treatment of hats, however, is not always advisable, and it is often worthwhile to send the hat to a cleaner and have it re-blocked.

DON BRADMAN'S SPECIAL HONOUR

Press report, Sydney. Don Bradman has achieved a new distinction – a place in the company of the famous people who have been commemorated **in English china**.

When the Australian team visited the Worcester Royal Porcelain factory last year, the directors mentioned that they intended to commemorate Don Bradman's unique feat of having made three double centuries in his last three visits to the Worcestershire ground.

As a result, a magnificent vase will be presented to Bradman after the South Australia v NSW match in Sydney this week. One side of the vase is painted with a view of Worcester Cathedral with a cricket pitch in the foreground and Don Bradman at the wicket. Bradman scored his runs in 1930, (236), 1934 (206), and 1938 (258).

As mementos of their visit, members of the Australian team will receive gilded porcelain plates bearing facsimiles of the team's signatures in gold.

STOP PRESS ON ECHIDNAS

News report, Melbourne. Melbourne echidnas or porcupines, which are more numerous in the metropolitan area at this season than at other times, puzzle the Chief Inspector of Fisheries and Game (Mr Lewis). Yesterday he had a phone call from a Brunswick woman who found one in her garden, and did not know what to do with it. The porcupines are not wanted by the Zoo.

Mr Lewis says they can be made into pets, but they have the disability of lacking any great brain power – "the brains of a worm" was the way he put it – and they **cannot be stroked**.

THE DRUNKOMETER IS COMING

Revelers might have trouble in future. It is reported that a treacherous piece of machinery has been invented in Indiana by Dr R Karger which, it is claimed, can measure the degree of intoxication in an alcohol drinker.

The drunkometer was this week demonstrated at the Victorian Option Alliance by Mrs G Waldeck, a lecturer in the Women's Christian Temperance Union. The suspect is allowed to blow into a balloon. The exact alcoholic content of his breath is then determined. It is said to be no use pretending to be too ill to blow up the balloon, as the machine is equipped with a device for extracting breath from the lungs.

Victorian police are requesting more information from American colleagues.

MARCH: CZECH RUMP FALLS

For the first ten days of March, the world looked a brighter place. **It was now six months since the Munich crisis, and overall, Hitler had behaved.** Of course he was still in the forefront in fomenting riots, and border disputes, and threats of violence all over Europe, and he was still the master of pugnacious insulting speeches. Still, there had been no real crisis, and the British were starting to breathe a little easier.

Letters to the papers were lightening up a little. There was a lot less talk about the certainty of war, and **even some frivolity of sorts was presented**.

Letters, Arthur Arnold. I have read with much interest the letters in *The Times* about the doodle oak. The pronunciation in the South of England is more commonly dottle, but the word has almost entirely gone out of use during the last 40 years. I think the correct definition of the doodle or dottle is that which is left, hence pollard. Boundary trees or stems are almost invariably pollards, not necessarily oak.

There are very large areas of woodlands in the South of England which are technically known as coppice with standards, in other words, trees with underwood growing under them. This underwood was cut periodically every eight or 10 years. It was customary to leave us a boundary between the cuttings - stems of underwood cut off about to 3ft high, which eventually grow large and were called dottles or doodles. In the same way a bound or a boundary oak or other tree was invariably pollarded, hence the word dottle or doodle. The man who lights up the old plug in his pipe without refilling is said to light the dottle in his pipe or that which is left.

Comment. Now that I've got that sorted out, we can go back to the war.

Other Letters, dealing with war matters, were not quite as doomsday as before.

Letters, Colonel E Carter. The Bishop of St David's quotes several reasons against a tank gunnery school in Pembrokeshire such as its being on most fertile agricultural land, its natural beauty, its sentimental and sacred associations with three parishes. Natural beauty, however, is not affected by tank gunnery; in fact, at Lulworth, where a similar agitation was staged some years ago, the gunnery ranges have preserved its natural condition and saved it from being ruined by the speculative builder. Both at Lulworth and the air ranges near Chesil Beach, wild birds are not affected by gunfire and breed freely on the ranges. Many soldiers will remember birds, particularly larks, singing continuously in the heaviest gunfire in France.

As to parishes, I know many in which their men were killed in 1915-1918 because, through their lack of training, they were ignorant of the necessary means of preserving their lives in the face of a better trained enemy. If the Bishop or anyone can suggest a better site, the War Office would certainly examine it, because they do not want the most fertile land, but in the meantime I am sure the rising tide of protest, which the Bishop hopes for, will not come from the men who may, for the protection of their country, have to face a well-trained and competent enemy in battle.

Letters, Troy Hardin. It was reported at a meeting of Beaconsfield Council last night that one of the biggest houses in the district had been excluded from the emergency evacuation returns to the Government as the owner had stated that all accommodation there had been reserved by the Government **for storing works of art**. The council decided to write to the Government asking them to revise that decision.

News Item. The Home Office, so far as possible, is **to avoid delivering air raid shelters on Mondays**. Many complaints were received yesterday that, on Mondays, washing was torn and dirtied in backyards and the day's routine upset by the delivery of shelters.

But sadly, **these better times would not last**. It took Hitler only one week to plunge the entire world back into an ever-conscious dread of war.

EVENTS IN CZECHOSLOVAKIA

First, a short lesson on geography. At the end of WWI, the Treaty of Versailles had imposed on Germany an **impossible set of rules** that right now she was breaking away from. Among these were that vast numbers of **German citizens** were no longer classified as Germans, but **were now Austrians, Czechs, or Poles**. These lands were all to the East of Germany, and bordering on that nation. Hitler had grabbed Austria for Germany a year ago. Then he had grabbed the Sudetenland from the Czechs six months ago, because it was full of Germans. But now, he decided to go one step further. **He wanted the remainder of Czechoslovakia.** And, let me state in advance, he got it, every bit of it.

He used tactics similar to those in his two previous adventures. Within Czechoslovakia, Slovakia was a separate State, just like Victoria is here. He encouraged nationalism there, and at the drop of Hitler's hat, that State declared its independence. The Czech central government moved troops in, to prevent this. After a couple of days' stand-off, Hitler called the Prime Minister of the Czechs, Hacha, to Berlin. There he presented him with the statement of fact that unless he consented to handing over his nation to Germany, Hitler would invade it at 6am next morning. Hacha had no military forces worth considering, and he signed the necessary papers. Because, after all, everything had to be done legally.

So, **Czechoslovakia ceased to exist**. Three States were created in its place, Croatia, a Czech State, and Ruthenia. But these were all now States of Germany. Various governments all over the world objected to all this, but as Hitler rejoiced "no one has mobilised against us." **Once again, he had played his game of bully and bluff, and once again, he had won.**

BRITISH REACTION

The British Government, along with the French, sent off notes of protest, temporarily withdrew their ambassadors, made diplomatic complaints, and used the normal range of **ineffectual remonstrations**. The German response, to criticism from half the nations of the world, was to reject the protests. In Britain's case, Hitler asked "What right does Britain have, with its vast Empire round the world, to complain about Germany absorbing a neighbour who wanted to be absorbed, and with a population of less than 10 million people?"

The public's reaction was summed up by this Letter below.

Letters, Robert Ashby. We have too long agonised over the harsh way we treated the Germans after Versailles. We all realise it was unrealistic to expect them to accept indefinitely that a third of their population was **by definition** now living in other countries, and that a proud nation could not have an effective Army, Navy, Air Force, ships, and submarines. We know we should have done more to fix this than the trifles we have done.

On the other hand, the solution to this is not the way Hitler has chosen. He could have waited a few years and mustered the support that was growing for his causes, and made his changes without the disasters he is now sure to cause. He could have, but he did not. We must accept that also.

Having recognised all of the above, we should forget how we got here. We are in an irretrievable situation. **Nothing we can do can stop war.** Hitler has burned his last boat, and England and France cannot turn another blind eye to the next transgression. The leaders in our democracies are so deeply caught up in this that they cannot say once more "it was an internal matter."

So forget how we got here. We need to concentrate on getting ourselves ready for **a certain war.** Nothing else should occupy out thoughts. We should go about our business with our customary aplomb, but with a hidden grim determination that we must stop this dictator in his tracks, and ensure that the principles we stand for continue to stand.

Mr Ashby's Letter reflected the national mood. All of a sudden, almost the entire population rallied behind the Parliamentary leadership. Neville Chamberlain for once got strong support from the Opposition when he said "enough is enough". **He was wildly cheered in Parliament** as he made many backs-to-the-wall defiant statements, and as he announced various immediate initiatives to increase wartime preparations. **It looked like Britain had toughened up, and really was getting ready to go to war.**

BACK IN OZ

Prime Minister Lyons was as worried as everyone else was. He commented "I must give expression to my profound disappointment and alarm at the events which have taken place in the last few days. We had assumed that the Munich Agreement had effected a settlement of the Czech question, and decided the extent of the occupation of that country. Instead, it is clear that the German government is effecting a military occupation of territory inhabited by people not of the German race. We look forward to the future with deep misgiving."

Lord Stanley Bruce, Australia's High Commissioner to Britain, weighed in with similar sentiments, and offered a strange mixture of **warning, and hope, and recrimination. Of warning,** he said "the immediate situation was dangerous and difficult beyond words". **Of hope,** "we can see it improving every day, and the danger will soon be survived." **Of recrimination,** "When Germany first advised that she was intended to defy the Versailles Treaty and rearm her military forces, she could have been brought to her knees in a few weeks."

Comment. There were many people in Oz who were not as sanguine about the daily improvements that were obvious to Lord Bruce.

Letter writers were very vocal. **The writer below** speaks below for most of them.

Letters, Talonis. The dissolution of Czechoslovakia and its absorption by the German Reich is too much of an accomplished fact for any protestations of horror or surprise to change it. The critics of the Munich Agreement have found that they have been amply justified by the recent course of events, and to-day Mr Chamberlain must be the most bitterly disappointed man in Europe. The spirit of Munich has not been kept.

It may be argued that the latest developments could not have possibly been foreseen last September. But surely it should have been obvious that the German demands for the incorporation of the Sudetenland within the Reich were prompted not so much by any altruistic motives towards the Sudetans, but rather by a desire to control the natural and highly fortified frontier behind which the Czechs have dwelt in security since the inception of their State.

Has the German expansion ended? Her frontiers virtually face Romania, and that country, rich in forests, agriculture, and above all, oil, is a prize which the German militarists will find all too tempting. The policy of appeasement has failed, and our attempts for peace, altruistic as they have been have been, interpreted as weakness. The decision rests with France and England.

Either they must be prepared to aid the smaller democracies in resisting the encroachments of the totalitarian states, else they must be prepared to face a Fascist Europe in which justice and the liberty of the subject have disappeared.

However, not everyone saw this situation through the same eyes. Below is correspondence from some quite rare dissenters.

Letters, Aryan, Clifton Hill. It is unfortunate that European problems are not viewed from two sides. Why are Hitler and Franco held up as wrongdoers? Has not Hitler every right to return Germany to her former greatness? Germany is a greater place today – no unemployment, housing conditions that are a lesson to all countries, and a will to improve themselves physically. (In Australia young men haunt pubs and waste money gambling every Saturday: not a few, but thousands.)

Hitler is the greatest figure in history. Consider what he has accomplished without war. (Napoleon is called great because he wasted millions of lives in a useless venture.) If England and France will not grant him the right to trade freely, he has to find his own methods. Hence the Eastern States of Europe, who will be better off under German domination. Austria, Vilna, Sudetenland, and the Polish are rightly German. Has Germany to depend on the handouts of England, like a humble dog? **The greatest crime in history was the Treaty of Versailles**, and the greatest criminal M. Clemenceau. The food blockade was continued for 12 months after the war, and thousands of Germans perished. This is a crime she has a right to avenge.

Letters, LCB, St Kilda. I admit that strict equality among nations is an unattainable ideal; but striving for partial attainment must be a better policy than doing nothing to relieve the tension. With all the trade agreements and preferential tariffs in force today Germany and Italy have not got equality of access to raw materials. Germany had to devote a large part of her income to rearmament, as while she was unarmed she got nowhere.

The blocking of Germany's and Italy's reasonable expansion will certainly cause war (with no real winners). If proper appeasement (not the past scratching-the-surface efforts) is tried there will be reasonable chance of avoiding the catastrophe. Assuming war comes, and we emerge victorious (by no means a foregone conclusion), we would most likely have the vicious cycle of the last 20 years over again – another Treaty of Versailles, with its natural repercussions. This method has been proved a failure, so why not give the alternative method of true appeasement a trial, even if it should mean the eventual swallowing up of the Balkans and the Ukraine?

OTHER DEFENCE MATTERS

There was no shortage of Letters offering suggestions as
to what should be done. The idea of issuing guns to large
numbers of people had a lot of supporters. But Askarri, of
Melbourne, pours cold water on the idea.

Letters, Askarri. In Thursday's issue you publish
another of the frequent suggestions that every citizen
be issued with a rifle and a hatful of ammunition
and let loose to "defend Australia". Those who
know the range and penetration of the service rifle
will shudder at the prospective slaughter of cows,
horses, and humans in the first week of issue. The
guerrilla army idea is picturesque, but dangerous
and the authorities should kill it before it further
misleads people. In the Palestine campaign we
frequently had the "support" of enthusiastic bands
of Arab irregulars. They were so "irregular" as to
be a constant menace to their allies.

Then there is this novel idea. A bit silly, most people
thought. So too did military men from the old school.

Letters, Alan Smith, Tamworth. I get worried
when I read of the way we are preparing for war.
Our papers are full of our horsemen in Brigades
going through their training, and we hear all sorts
of talk about how well these Brigades performed in
the Great War.

But look at Hitler's great parades. You will see
aeroplanes, and giant cannons, and especially
tanks. There will be no room for horses. These
modern tanks can destroy horse brigades easily,
and today's fighters can kill a hundred horses with
one pass over. Cannons can kill another hundred

from a distance of 10 miles. We do not need to buy and supply food for horses. What we need is to provide petrol for tanks, and ammunition for big guns, and bombs for planes. Then we have a chance of not being slaughtered.

BIRTH RATES IN AUSTRALIA

Letters, Australian parent. The subject of our declining birth rate has been touched on frequently in the Press, yet practically no notice has been taken of it by those in authority. Is it because the subject has no vote-catching appeal? Surely we have some leaders with a national outlook.

Letters, E Manton. The low birth rate is a matter demanding immediate attention. For the last ten years it has been below replacement rate, 200 per 10,000 of population. Our native-born population must begin to decrease unless something is done. A campaign to educate married couples **on their duty to the State** and a **ban on the sale of contraceptives** would do much to remedy the position. To talk of White Australia is farcical if we cannot populate it. The population of Japan is increasing at the rate of 1 million per year.

Letters, G Robinson. Ivanhoe. Women employed in jobs which could be filled by men and lads have no desire to have children with the result that there is no home life such as existed in the good old days when large families were the order for the best of families. The good time that the women of to-day look for and obtain soon leads them to the divorce court.

Here are my remedies. **First**, throw all female employees out of work where the work can be done by males. **Second**, give all married couples with six children a pension to help support them. **Third**, exempt from taxation all parents having 10 children still living. **Fourth**, increase the workers' wages and standards of living 50 per cent at least. **Fifth**, prevent profiteering by establishing a fair profits and fair rents court. **Sixth**, make divorce easy for a man prepared to have a family if his spouse refuses.

WHITE AUSTRALIA POLICY

Letters, C Mansfield. The White Australia Policy has proved to be one of Australia's greatest mistakes. It still is, and although we refuse to consider it, we shall probably be compelled, in view of the world position, to show how we propose to maintain it.

Our far North country is many times larger than the British Isles, and has been left unpopulated and undefended. And why? Because, on the one hand, it is impossible, owing to the tropical state, for white people to handle under the present existing economic conditions, and on the other hand, because the White Australia Policy prevents the importation of coloured people capable of working under such climatic conditions. Could anything be more ludicrous than for seven million people holding out an obvious challenge to the rest of the world.

Letters, Bryson Wilson. We are behaving like a bunch of school kids. The best thing that could possibly happen to Australia would be a sudden invasion. It would wake the people up, and then, in all probability, a real leader would appear in place of all these lifeless and most expensive governments. We need a leader as much as we need anything, even if it is a dictator. This major problem has to be tackled.

If we intend to populate the far north and to hold it, then we must immediately scrap the White Australia Policy. We must establish sufficient inducement to people, regardless of colour, to emigrate under Australian laws. Yes, it's no doubt drastic, but the alternative is that we shall lose our empty spaces, and we deserve to.

Letters, John Holder. The Australian Government should put up signs right along the coast, from Perth, to Darwin, to Cairns. They should be 20 miles apart.

They should say: *This is white Australia. Coloured people keep out.*

TV FOR OZ?

The Chairman of Amalgamated Wireless in Australia, AWA, Sir Ernest Fisk, said that there were problems associated with the production of TV for commercial purposes.

He explained that TV sets cost 26 guineas to 60 guineas in Britain. The most expensive showed a picture of only 10 inches by 8 inches, while the cheap sets showed 5 by 3. Few people would sit looking at such a small screen.

The only source from which TV broadcasts could be drawn regularly was the motion picture film, which cost from 10,000 to 20,000 Pounds to make. The makers recovered the cost by admittance charges to picture theatres. **How could the cost of a film made for TV be recovered?** Broadcasting ranges were severely limited. After TV had been in practice for three years in Britain, the reliable range of transmission was from five to 30 miles. Although 8 million persons were within the range of the London transmitting station, only 10,000 homes had been equipped for reception. **This would be far less in Australia.**

At present there is no substantial demand in Britain. Makers who could turn out from 20,000 to 30,000 sets per week, are producing only 400. Therefore, he said, **it will be ten years before commercial TV sets were available in Australia.**

Comment. He was pretty accurate, allowing for the War. . In fact, TV effectively came here only in time for the 1956 Melbourne Olympics.

SOAP-BOX RACING

Letters, K White, Collingwood Boys Settlement. I have read in your paper that Mr Bedford is having made in Sydney an expensive all-steel streamlined soap-box to be entered in the derby to be held at St Kilda on April 1. My friends and I in Collingwood have been making soap-boxes for many years, and we don't believe his jib will have any advantage over our wooden hand-made carts.

Our experience has shown us how to make and how to drive a soap-box, and Mr Bedford would probably be surprised at the fast trials we have made. I am not able to disclose the details now, but the Collingwood entrants are confidently looking forward to the tussle.

CAGED COCKIES

Letters, Aged bird lover. Last Sunday week I visited the Zoo and was shocked to see one of the beautiful cockatoos struggling along the floor of its cage with a brass ring round its leg holding it in place. I not only pointed this out to the man at the gate, but also wrote to the curator of the Gardens. My letter was ignored. If the authorities controlling the Zoo are going to allow such disgraceful treatment to exist, the sooner the birds are liberated the better, or given to some-one who will treat them kindly.

SNAKES ALIVE

News report. Wangaratta. While clearing away debris piled up against a fence by floodwaters from the Horseshoe Creek, Misses Nellie, Mollie, and Elizabeth Milye, of Milawa, unexpectedly found themselves in a nasty snake-killing exercise.

One of the sisters was clearing away some of the debris, when a snake wriggled out. She promptly killed it. Investigating further, she saw several other snakes, and sought the assistance of her sisters. They found that the debris was literally alive with snakes, and they killed one after another until they had accounted for 304. The snakes were of various kinds and sizes.

SOLDIERS' PREFERENCE

Letters, Private rank. I wish to protest at the present system of preference to returned soldiers from WWI. I was too young even when War had ceased, so why should I be penalised? Granted returned soldiers left positions to fight for our heritage, does not 20 years' lapse give us the equal right to live and exist in our own country? If war ever comes again, it is we who will have to carry on the same heritage.

WE BUILD PLANES NOW

Australia's first home-built plane, the Wirraway, easily went through its trials at the end of March. It was reported "to have passed with flying colours. It will now be put into production at a high rate."

As it turned out, the Wirraway was valuable for transporting men and equipment and the like. But it was too slow and stiff for air battles, and was no match for sleeker overseas products, like the Japanese Zeroes.

MENZIES' UNIVERSAL HEALTH INSURANCE

Bob Menzies, the Attorney General of the nation, had been proposing a **universal** health insurance plan for the population. However, this plan was defeated by Parliament, which elected to go instead for a **reduced** health insurance scheme. As a consequence, **Mr Menzies has resigned his position, and will now join the Back Bench**.

APRIL: BRITAIN TRIES MORE TREATIES

Neville Chamberlain really must have been about the most disappointed man in Europe. After all, last September he arrived back in England with the scrap of paper, signed by Hitler, promising that there would be no more takeovers of territory. He had dined out on that for six months, telling everyone that Hitler wanted peace, and could be managed. **Now**, it was obvious that Hitler **wanted more living space to the East**, and **that** was higher up his priority list than peace was. If he had to, he could do without peace.

So Chamberlain had to come to terms with watching the Czechs being routed, and succumbing to German rule. Then, a few days later, Hitler pulled off another, smaller, coup in Lithuania. This latter country was a State on the Baltic Sea, half way to Russia. The principal city, and only real port, was at Memel, and over 90 per cent of the population there were German.

By now, you know what that means. For months, Hitler had been sending his riotous Nazi patriots there under cover, and had also been smuggling in armaments of all sorts. After the Czech fiasco, Hitler sailed on the battleship, *Deutschland*, and landed at Memel. There, the welcome in the streets was rapturous.

Over the next few weeks, the Nazis took over the various functions and positions in the government of Memel, and ultimately gained full control of that city. The whole manoeuvre was nicely orchestrated, almost bloodless. Overall, it was important because it signaled to everyone, including Britain and Chamberlain, that Hitler had not reached the end of his ambitions after Czechoslovakia, and that in all probability he still had a few more tricks up his sleeve.

But, in any case, **his good mate Mussolini was quite capable of adding some ginger to the mix**. Albania was a small nation on the other side of the Adriatic from Italy. It was a simple, unambitious nation on the world stage, and was very dependent on Italy for its economy. But it had its own King and Queen and its own army, and its own pride. None of this deterred Mussolini, and in early April he invaded that nation. There was some small gallant resistance from the army, but it was crushed fully in a couple of days, the King and Queen fled to Greece, and **Benito was free to provide his protection and his troops to that lucky nation**.

Here again was a **follow-up copy-cat demonstration** of the **right of might**. Once again, **there was no move from anywhere to intervene,** and a shell-shocked Europe and England realised even more clearly that war was almost certain. Even die-hard pacifists were finding it hard to deny.

CHAMBERLAIN'S NEXT MOVES

Immediately after the demise of Czechoslovakia, Chamberlain and his Cabinet spent a week talking about treaties of various sorts with the central European nations to somehow convince them that they would not get similar treatment. So, his Government gave military guarantees to Poland, Romania, Greece and Turkey.

Later, it talked for a week about a Grand Alliance, between the non-Hitler nations, aimed at defence against Hitler. It was like a small League of Nations, cooked up in a week, but fortunately, good sense prevailed and it died a rapid and deserved death.

Colonel Rochester, of Warwick, had something to say about the various treaty proposals.

I have watched Governments for half a century sign treaties, pacts, concordats, trade alliances, non-aggression compacts, agreements, and the like. Most of them were ignored or abrogated when the occasion suggested it.

In today's world, the urge to write such useless documents is greater than ever. It is nice for a politician to be able to say, at the end of the day, I am not helpless, and boast of getting something signed. But our politicians right now are helpless. They can talk to Poland, Russia, Romania and Greece, but in the long run, every one of these countries will do what is in their own interests, and those interests alone. This **was** not always the case, but it is true today.

The only procedure that has any meaning today is when a democratically-elected Government says loudly and clearly that it will do such and such, and the people support this. Then, and only then, will the promise be kept. The guarantee then comes from the will of the people, and not the varying moods and perceptions and guiles of politicians and diplomats.

COMPULSORY MILITARY TRAINING

Late in April, Prime Minister Chamberlain introduced Bills into parliament that approved the introduction of **compulsory military training for males aged 20 to 21**.

The males would be moved to military camps for a period of three months, and on completion of the basic training, remain in reserve forces for a period of about three years. During that time, they would attend drill sessions each month and a short camp each year.

These were controversial Bills. The British Government had promised for years that compulsion would never be used **in peacetime**, and yet now it had reneged on that promise. Chamberlain went to some lengths to explain that while the nation was clearly not at war, that everyone knew that the situation was very volatile, and the outbreak of hostilities could come at any time. "Anti-aircraft gunners need to be trained and that takes a lot more time than we might have."

Most of the population supported the Bills. There was dissent from the Labour Party, the Opposition. This Party was very divided on the issue. Clement Attlee, its Leader, opposed the Bills on the argument that compulsion was not legitimate in a democratic society in a time of peace. Others in the Party, though voting against the Bills, privately supported them, on the basis that it was obvious that trained men were needed in the current circumstance. Given the split within the Labour Party on the issue, their opposition was weak and ineffectual. The Bills passed into law without trouble.

Letters, ANXIOUS, London. I am in favour of conscription for three main reasons. **The first** is that it shows to the world our determination to stop the expansion of the Fascist States. **Second**, it is essential we have trained men not merely in a few months, but in a few days. **Third**, conscription is regarded across Europe as being democratic, and we are the only country here who does not have it.

But I am opposed to it as proposed by the Government. The number of men called up is too few, and **the list of reserved occupations is amazing**. Then there are supporting measures, such as the long delay in a shelter policy, and the lack of plans for food production and storage. These, and other measures, are just as essential as the military training of just a few youths.

We need to seriously address the issue of collective security by appointing a War Cabinet dedicated to matters of war and war only.

Letters, R Gamble. We send you the following as it may be of interest to you. As a result of the Cabinet's decision, we asked 100 members of our staff, taken at random, "Are you in favour of conscription?" The result showed 63 voted in favour, and 37 against. Our staff consisted of mechanics under 30, employed on the production of number plates. Most of them would be called up in an emergency.

THE THREAT FROM INCENDIARY BOMBS

Explaining why the public should be prepared for dealing with incendiary bombs, **a handbook, issued by the Government to all households**, states that one large bomber can carry between 1,000 and 2,000 small bombs, which, if scattered over built-up areas and not dealt with within two or three minutes after falling, might start so many fires that no fire brigade could be expected to deal with them all. Moreover, water mains might be damaged or drained dry, or damaged roads might prevent a fire engine reaching the site.

The incendiary bomb most likely to be used, on account of its effectiveness is, according to the handbook, the light magnesium electron bomb, which weighs about 2lb. 2oz. These bombs would probably be dropped from a great height since they do not reach their maximum power of penetration until they have fallen about 5,000ft. Because of their lightness they cannot be aimed accurately. They spread out as they fall, and a group of bombs dropped simultaneously from 5,000ft would cover an area of about 100 yards square.

STEEL SHELTERS FOR BACKYARDS

The British Government announced at the end of the month that 60,000 shelters per week were being delivered to households in susceptible areas.

MR LYONS DIES IN SYDNEY

Friday, April 8. Press report. After a series of heart attacks, which began early on Thursday afternoon and continued through the night, **the Prime Minister (Mr Lyons) died** at St Vincent's private hospital, Darlinghurst at 10.40am today.

All night long Mr Lyons made a desperate fight for life. Even when the doctors in attendance felt that they could do no more, his resistance continued. Oxygen was administered at 4am, but the heart attacks continued until the end. Dame Enid Lyons was at the bedside, members of his family, Cabinet Ministers, and other close friends, were present in the hospital from where Sir Earle Page announced the death to the nation.

There will be a Requiem Mass on Tuesday, after which the State funeral cortège will proceed from St Mary's to Circular Quay, where the remains will be placed aboard a destroyer and taken to Devonport, Tasmania.

News of the Prime Minister's passing evoked a remarkable flood of expressions of sorrow from all sections of the community, emphasising his widespread personal popularity. Messages of sympathy have been received from all over the world. These include personal cables from the King and the Governor-General Designate (the Duke of Kent).

Sir Earle Page has accepted a commission to form a government. He was sworn in this afternoon as Prime Minister. His tenure of office will, however, be temporary, and has been arranged so that the administration of the Commonwealth may be carried on undisturbed. A new Prime Minister will probably take office in about two weeks or thereabouts.

My Lyons is the first Australian Prime Minister to die while in office. Had he lived until April 23 he would have exceeded by one day of service the record established by Mr W M Hughes.

Only today was it revealed that he had decided to retire soon from the leadership of the Government. His long and arduous term of office had begun to affect his general health, and he recently discussed his future with intimate friends and made it clear that he would shortly retire, probably at the time of the next election.

THE NEXT PRIME MINISTER

The Government of Australia was, at this time, in the hands of a Coalition that was dominated by the United Party, with the Country Party very much the junior partner. With the death of Joe Lyons, tensions within the Coalition turned into open hostility and, after a week of bitter fighting, the Country Party withdrew. **The United Party had the numbers to form Government in their own righ**t, and elected **Robert Gordon Menzies** as their leader, and he then accepted the position of **Prime Minister.**

Comment. This change in leadership, as we will see, meant **a much more aggressive approach towards preparing the nation for war**. Also, the split with the Country Party left the United Party with a reduced majority, and this would have its effects that will also become apparent in due course.

It is impossible to know what would have happened to Australia if Mr Lyons had not died when he did. You will remember that Menzies had been the Deputy Leader of the United Party until two weeks earlier, and had resigned over a health insurance issue. Without Mr Lyon's untimely death, it could be that Menzies would have sat unnoticed on the Back Bench until he passed into oblivion. Then this nation's history could well have been very different.

OTHER OZ WAR NEWS AND VIEWS

The news from England, late in the month, that limited conscription had been passed into law, would surely influence public opinion in Australia. Apart from the "we follow England" effect, there was the same sure logic at work in both places.

Meanwhile, **Letter-writers and events** kept crowding in.

Letters, H Tonkin. The conversion of electric tram services to that of the motor-bus might well be considered as an important factor in national defence. Buses could be constructed into semi-armored cars by means of steel shutters to cover windows making them practically bullet-proof. This service would overcome the danger of bombing of crowded troop and passenger trains. A rapid ready-made means of transport with a minimum of risk.

Letters, W Maloney, MP for Melbourne. I desire, through the courtesy of your columns, to make an appeal to the citizens of Australia that it would be worthy of consideration of the Commonwealth and States to form a Foreign Legion for training refugees who are only too willing to come to our shores and help fill our empty spaces.

The Legion would have to be formed on the principle of the Foreign Legion as carried out in France and Europe, which would enable legionnaires to swear immediate allegiance to the Australian Government and so avoid having to **wait for the five years before they were naturalised.**

If this were done, I feel compelled to consider we could soon form an army of trained men who would fight for this country as their home against Nazi and Fascist ideals. It could be made a condition permitting their entry into Australia that after two or three years of service they would be entitled to become citizens of the Commonwealth.

PROSPECTS FOR WAR: THE GERMAN VIEW

The Consul-General for Germany in Australia, Dr R Amis, speaking in Fremantle on April 18, said:

"I have found that a proper understanding of European affairs is lacking among many Australians. As I have travelled in Australia, I have had the impression that many Australians believe that there will be war. **I do not believe that there will be war**. I do not see any reason for war, at least as far as Germany is concerned. I do not believe that Germany will go to war to press her claims, and I do not believe she will go into Poland.

"I see in the establishment of a protectorate over the Czechs simply as a reaction against rearmament by Great Britain. You know, **Britain has started an encirclement policy round Germany** and the Axis powers had to act against it. Hence the occupation of Albania.

"I think that Germany is now satisfied with the position, except with regard to the colonies. But there will be no war over these. The whole German population had seen, in the Munich Agreement, the first step towards a solid friendship with the British Empire, and it is very disappointing to them that the only reply has been the enormous rearmament programme of Britain. The race for arms in Europe is very regrettable, but from our point of view, we have to protect ourselves when threatened.

"But, to sum up, I do not believe that Germany will go to war to press her claims. I do not believe she will go into Poland. There will be no war for the colonies."

Comment. These were reassuring words, and they represented the official German line. But they were hard to believe, given the day-to-day provocations that the Nazis were offering all over Europe, and their own enormous build-up of military strength, well in excess of the British.

It is interesting that this statement was not considered at all important, and was buried on Page 18 of *The Argus*.

KEEP WOMEN IN THEIR PLACE

All women should be womanly, according to an address given to the Town and Country Women's Club tonight by Dr A Vattuone, of Brisbane. Outside the home and the school, he said, women should not work at all.

A woman sitting all day long at a desk or on a judge's bench, or working in an operating theatre or as a policewoman or woman soldier can be very useful, but she is no longer a woman. She cannot be a wife and she cannot be a mother, because she has lost her femininity, and emancipation has made her masculine.

Bad diet, insufficient food, slimming ideas, starvation, intoxication of any sort, and especially the abuse of tobacco and liquor, diminish and destroy femininity.

There are some women, fortunately very few, who, having formed the habit of continuous daily smoking and drinking as a hobby, should, for their own safety and that of the race, be placed in special restraining institutions. They are not feminine.

In the same way, Dr Vattuone continued, by many occupations and by unreasonable strains, the femininity of a lot of modern girls was spoiled. Girls too ambitious in sports underwent very heavy training in jumping, foot-running, swimming, etc, without any care at all for their feminine characteristics. They ended by upsetting their normality, and in sick moments they abused such things as aspirin and gin. They became athletic and masculine, and a woman with a masculine mind was as anomalous a creature as a woman with a man's muscular arms and legs or a man's beard .

Famous women, Dr Vattuone added, were not at all common, but famous women who had at the same time been happy and loving mothers were very little known in history. Almost all had paid for their attempts by a bad nervous state and by suffering from chronic neurasthenia.

Letters, A NEUTER BEING. No doubt there is much truth in Dr Vattuone's statement that too much freedom has turned the modern woman into what is best described as a neuter being. Nevertheless, if they have lost their femininity, they carry on in their jobs very efficiently.

And what of modern man? World conditions are solely in the hands of males, and there is abundant evidence to-day that proves that they have not made a great success of their responsibilities, be their nationalities what they may.

Letters, LOOKER-ON. How many times is the smoking and alcohol saturated woman preferred as a wife to the refined and home-loving one who would be willing to bring up a family? Hundreds of these good women are passed by because they will not display themselves like the above-mentioned ones do. Is it not possible to educate our young men to realise their responsibilities to the nation?

Far too much time is spent by women with sport, and I think that young women should be debarred from winning a prize or trophy in any kind of sport. Also, no married woman should be sent overseas by any sporting body.

Comment. Dr Vattuone's strong opinions were so provocative that they were presented on the front page of *The Argus*. Still, there were large numbers in society, men and women, who supported his views, more or less.

OLDER CHILDREN ARE DUMB?

Letters, SCHOOL TEACHER. I was surprised to read that your correspondent GJ finds difficulty in **accepting the fact that younger members of families are mentally superior to their older brothers and sisters**.

I am one of those teachers and I can assure GJ that in very many cases I have found the oldest children below average intelligence, sometimes almost subnormal, **each child an improvement in every way on his immediate elder**, and, if the family be large enough, the younger ones distinctly above the average.

The reason for this is certainly not that the younger children are better looked after or better nourished – it must, I think, be biological. I have never known the converse to be true.

I should like to point out, too, that we teachers know it is not economic difficulties that lessen the size of families. Parents who are very comfortably off, in a position to go away for holidays, play golf, or bridge, with fervour, have a miserable **only**

child or none at all (children are a drawback when holidaying or enjoying some sport), while poor parents have large families – and the larger the family the better the children.

DECLINING BIRTH RATES

Letters, VERB SAP. The low birth rate, like most of out other economic ills, is brought about largely by well-meaning but foolish legislation. One chief example is the law that women and girls may be paid at lower rates of wages than men and boys. When this came into force, the banks, shops, and offices began to fill up with girls, where previously boys had been engaged. The boys, being thus left out in the cold, were unable to marry the girls and raise families.

If this were reversed, and **the rates for women and girls were made higher than those for men and boys**, the result would be marked and immediate. The boys would get the jobs, and the girls would get husbands. What about it?

Comment. Pay girls more than boys? Interesting idea.

Letters, F Piersen. I married before I was 20 years of age, and my wife gave birth to 10 children (all single births) before either of us was 37 years old. During that time none of these children brought home any money. I was never out of work, but was so poor that I have had to keep in bed on Sunday mornings while my shirt was washed. At that time one could buy a new shirt for a shilling. You will understand what a struggle we had, and I am not surprised at the declining birth rate.

MAY: EUROPE AFTER THE CZECHS

A revisionary lesson in history and geography. Germany, as a single State, did not exist prior to 1870. At that date, it was "unified", so that a number of "races" all came under control of a single Government. For example, in the Eastern areas of the new nation there were large communities, each numbering tens of millions, of people who were of Polish, or Germanic, or Prussian origin.

After the Treaty of Versailles, new boundaries were drawn all over the world, and as part of that, **the State of Poland was re-created right in the middle of the Eastern provinces of Germany.** This meant that East Prussia was cut off from that Germany by hundreds of miles, but it still remained a State of that fair land. At the same time, a major German port, Danzig, 90 per cent populated by Germans, was given to Poland.

So the **Polish race** ended up with what it wanted. That is, its own territory, and its own Government, and even the official control of a new valuable German asset, the important port of Danzig.

Europe after Czechoslovakia. Nobody in Europe thought for one minute that Hitler had been mollified by his Czech coup. So the race for everyone to sign treaties with everyone else was really on. For example, Poland was sometimes talking, and sometimes not talking, to Britain, and France, as well as Germany, as well as Russia and Turkey. Britain was doing likewise with Russia, who was doing likewise with Germany, who in turn really sometimes wanted alliances with Britain. Some of this is shown in the typical daily headlines given overleaf. **Ignore the detail, and just recognize the perfidy in all this.**

A DAY IN EUROPE

The London *Times* published a summary column under that heading of *A Day in Europe.* On May 16th it produced a typical summary, and I offer it here to give you an idea of what the average Britisher was digesting daily.

Again, don't worry about the detail. Look instead at the scope of the news and the subdued fear behind it.

Czech Nationalists distributed leaflets among crowds in Prague yesterday. The leaflets exhorted the Czech people to remain steady in the belief that their country would be freed.

> *"Remember always that you are Czechs," they read. "Turn your thoughts back to the history of your State." They instructed the Czechs about the attitude they should adopt toward German soldiers occupying the former Czech Republic. "Be correct in your behaviour," they said. "But remember that they are foreign troops."*

Herr Hitler, *accompanied by the chief of the secret police (Herr Himmler),* **began a tour of the German fortifications today.** *He and his party inspected the new defences at Aachen, 45 miles west-south-west of Cologne, which were originally excluded from the Siegfried line, but have been built up in the last few months into what is claimed to be an impregnable wall of steel and concrete.*

Il Duce's (Mussolini) speech at Turin yesterday *is regarded as pacific and moderate by diplomatic officials in London. His statement that there are no questions in*

Europe of such magnitude as to justify a general war is interpreted as having left the door open for a peaceful settlement.

The Times *takes a favourable view of the speech. It says that, although there was much in it that was couched in a challenging tone, it is not felt that it will leave European relations any worse off than they were before.*

A more critical note is struck by the **"Daily Telegraph,"** *which says that there is a bitter, ironic humour in the fact that the democracies are being reproached with not being sincerely devoted to peace. The humour is more bitter and ironic, it continues, when its author is a leader who boasts of the Italian subjugation of Abyssinia and the "union" of Albania and Italy.*

Official circles in Berlin *express complete approval in every respect with the speech. An intimation to this effect was given by a spokesman for the German Foreign Office last night.*

Paris remains unimpressed by the speech. *Madame Tabouis, in an article in "L'Oeuvre," expresses the opinion that the conclusion of the Anglo-Turkish pact caused Il Duce to moderate his remarks at the eleventh hour.*

There is much comment among officials in Belgrade, the capital of Yugoslavia, about **the Anglo-Turkish pact,** *which is regarded as a great triumph for British diplomacy. It is believed that it will exercise a decisive influence upon the foreign policy of Balkan countries.*

The Turkish Government *has given an order for British railway rolling stock worth 500,000 Pounds. This is the first result of the British credit of 16,000,000 Pounds granted to*

Turkey last year. In the meantime it is reported that Turkey has postponed the signing of a German contract to build a naval base in the Sea of Marmara.

A warning not to give way to German demands *on the colonial question was uttered last night by Viscount Stonehaven, formerly Governor-General of Australia. Lord Stonehaven was speaking at Oxford.*

He said that it was useless to believe that peace would be preserved by giving way. "You will never buy Herr Hitler off. You will never get anywhere by handing over colonies.

*"The most you will do is postpone war, and when war comes you will find yourselves in an immeasurably weakened position. But if Germany forces the issue today she will find that we are five times as formidable as we were in 1914, and **if there is a war there can be no doubt about how it will end.**"*

Japan has imposed a blockade on all foreign shipping in its occupied waters. *This will certainly appear to apply to all British shipping, and more details are being requested.*

Comment. What a hurly burly. A world just entering a stage of madness.

BRITISH NEWS AND TRIVIA

Letters, Commander G Marshall, None Go By, Burnt Mill Road, North Benfleet, Essex. How are important civilian workers, particularly those in factories producing food or war supplies, going to get to work if war comes? A single enemy bomb can cripple transport services – particularly those depending on electricity, and prevent thousands of people from carrying on. Moreover, even if all were quiet, shortage of fuel owing to military requirements would greatly reduce normal transport facilities.

As one who has seen warfare in many parts of the world in the past 25 years, and has seen some 250 air raids in Spain alone, I maintain that **our old friend the bicycle is the answer to the enemy**.

I would suggest to members of ARP committees up and down the country that a bicycle is as essential a part of the equipment of every citizen as a respirator. The cyclist can go round bomb craters which would bring four-wheeled traffic to a standstill, and can take circuitous routes to work avoiding traffic blocks of military or ambulance convoys. If there are not enough bikes for everyone, we could have a supply of town bikes ready for use.

Letters, W Arner, Sandown, Ankle Hill, Melton Mowbray, Leicester.   In your recent columns, the Rev H Wilson claimed that Chesterfield pork pies are now rivaling those of Melton Mowbray. He even claimed precedence for Chesterfield pies long before those of Melton Mowbray. While I do not hold that Melton has any monopoly or special secret for the manufacture of this delicacy, I do maintain that Melton was the first place to start the trade in them, which has now reached such large proportions. Soon after the railway first came to Melton about 1847 there was a small shopkeeper in Leicester Street of this town whose wife, the daughter of a farmer, had been taught at home on the farm to enclose pork in pastry at pig-killing time every autumn. A lodger of this worthy couple, who worked on the new railway, suggested that he might be able to sell these pork pies to travellers on the railway, and that, as far as is known, was the commencement of pork pie making as a commercial proposition. It is a fact that advertisements are often to be seen in our local paper asking for men with the necessary skill for hand-raising pork pies. These have spread all over the country, and thus in large industrial centres you occasionally see a properly made pork pie, judged even by our highest standards. At a low estimate, 25 tons of pork pies leave this town every Christmas and are sent all over the country.

AUSTRALIAN MILITARY NEWS

Air Force press release. Authorities today revealed that the Bristol Beaufort Bomber, the fastest twin-engine bomber in any country, is now ready for production in large quantities, and it will be built both **here** and in Britain.

Many aircraft could possibly be needed in Britain, and if that is the case, some will be transferred from here to there. Others will remain in this sphere of activity, and will fly to units in the Far East.

The new bomber is designed for use as a bomber, torpedo-bomber, and as a long-range general reconnaissance aircraft. While details cannot be given, it can be revealed that it has a top speed of 292 mph, and that it is designed to carry a crew of four. It has a mechanical gun amidships, and carries other guns forward.

Comment. Although there was much commentary on the slowness of our preparations for war, some very useful things were happening. These were often in matters where the military could proceed without too much Governmental involvement.

VOTES FOR YOUTHS

The Premier of **Tasmania** announced that those "young men **under 21** years of age, who had recently joined the militia, will be eligible to vote in the State elections. If young men are prepared to undergo training to defend their country, surely they are entitled to have a voice in how they should be governed."

The Commonwealth will not follow Tasmania's lead. Mr Menzies said that "it is not a case of defence. It is a case of knowledge, experience, wisdom, and sense. Some young men might have these attributes. And equally, some older voters might not. But most of the young men clearly do not, and it would be foolish to give them a say."

PRAY FOR THE EMPIRE

In response to a request by the Prime Minister (Mr Menzies), tomorrow will be observed throughout the Commonwealth as a National Day of Prayer. The day has been chosen as the Sunday before Empire Day (May 24).

In making his suggestion to the heads of the Churches, Mr Menzies said, "Empire Day seems to me to provide an opportunity for reflecting on our history, a proper pride in the good things that we have been able to contribute to the world, and a chastened penitence for our errors.

"Above all, we must on these anniversary days dedicate ourselves anew to the way of justice and the keeping of the peace. These are not only magnificent political ideals. They are among the cardinal articles of our religious faith.

On behalf of the Commonwealth Government, I suggest that on Sunday, May 21, as the Sunday before Empire Day, the various Churches in Australia should in their services, pay special attention to this great theme, **dwelling upon the responsibilities of the Empire, rather than upon the glory**, and emphasising that lasting peace can be established only upon a foundation of good faith, good will, honour and understanding."

Comment. Mr Menzies, a fervent patriot, felt free to express himself with such sincerity because he was surrounded here by a nation that was just as patriotic.

FEAR OF THE NAZIS

Rabbi Freedman said today that **fear of the Nazis was still with almost every refugee who came to Australia**. He appealed to the Commonwealth Government to take adequate steps to protect refugee migrants from coercion by the German Government or its representatives.

For months he had been given to understand that refugee migrants in Perth from Germany, and countries under its control, were being watched by Nazi representatives and were expected to keep in touch with German consulates, he said. They were fearful of taking an indiscreet step, because they did not wish ill to befall relatives in the German-occupied countries they had left.

The petition to the Prime Minister, asking that refugees be allowed to serve in defence of Australia, originated, said Rabbi Freedman, among male refugees in Western Australia who at first hesitated because, if names were divulged, they knew how dreadful would be the punishment of their relatives. He felt that German Nazis were very active here, doing all they could to sabotage the movement of refugees into Australia.

He was convinced that anonymous letters received by Perth business men threatening them with unfortunate consequences if they employed refugees had come from a local Nazi source. There was a Nazi organisation in Perth.

BING AND FRANK
What's happening to good music?

"Crooning is like a dog whining at the moon, while so called hot rhythm takes people back to the days of opium dens and the Negroes," the Secretary of **Melbourne University's Conservatorium of Music**, Mr J Sutton, said last night.

"I have set my face against the abomination which has come into the country, and as far as I am concerned, their records should be smashed, censored and not admitted to fair Australia."

Mr Sutton deplored the fact that children were compelled to listen day after day to music which, to his mind, was developed from the lowest animal instincts. Everywhere he went, he added, he preached the gospel against crooning, and urged that children should be given the benefit of the best music they could get.

Comment. Despite such views, teen-age girls kept following Sinatra in their bobby-sox, and swooning at his voice. While their mothers got all dreamy-eyed when Crosby crooned his melodies for them.

THE START OF THE POST-WAR BUTTER WARS
Letters, Leslie Tulloh, Kew. The catch-cry has been used **that margarine is a product of black**

labour. Surely it is time these stupid antagonisms ceased. Much margarine is made from Australian beef fats. The proportion made from coconut oil is not high, and the **natives in the Pacific Islands, where the copra is produced,** are buying increasing quantities of Australian products, and are also British subjects. The responsibility for the increased sales of margarine is probably largely due to the wives of farmers not being allowed to sell dairy butter, and the forcing up of the price of butter generally. Those requiring cooking butter were driven to use margarine.

TOO MANY BACHELORS

Reverend B O'Farrell, at a Carmelite Communion breakfast at Middle Park yesterday, opined that "the life of a bachelor was generally a selfish one. Happy and contented homes were needed in Australia, and they could best be attained by young people marrying. **Young men should regard marriage as a vocation** and not as a hindrance to life."

It was agreed at the meeting to enter an emphatic protest against the proposed establishment of birth control clinics in industrial areas.

JUNE: THE JEWISH PROBLEM

For five years, Hitler and the Nazis had been progressively persecuting Jews inside Germany with more and more vigour. They began formally with the Nuremberg Law of 1935, when all Jews lost their citizenship and were declared subjects of the State. After that, Jews were classified according to such things as how much Aryan blood they had inherited, how Jewish was their husband or wife, their occupation, and where they lived. Then, they were persecuted accordingly. Some people saw the writing on the wall and left the country earlier. The US got many of its atomic scientists this way.

But most stuck around, because they had houses, jobs and families in Germany. Gradually, they were hounded. Some were bashed, some were put in prison, some had their wealth appropriated, most were forced to wear a coloured star that indicated they were Jewish. Some were herded into concentration camps, and many were executed. None were ignored.

This month, it was the Polish Jews inside Germany who got the special treatment.

Press report. Polish Jews throughout Germany have been notified by the Government that they must leave the country. Fifteen thousand Jews, and 3,000 Jews of Polish origin who have no country, must leave before the end of July. At Munich, 4,000 Jews have been arrested pending immediate deportation. At Dresden and other cities, the time-limit expires at noon tomorrow. Twenty-five thousand Jews from Vienna have already crossed the border, and will be placed in camps and similarly processed.

Press report. The German liner, *St Louis*, messaged to say that she will be returning to Hamburg today. She has been loitering off the coast of Cuba for over a week, waiting for port authorities to allow her to enter.

On board are 900 German refugees, mainly Jews, who have been told by the Government that they will have to pay $500 each before they can land. Also, they will have to post a bond that guarantees they will be able to pay their maintenance fees in a concentration camp. Most of them cannot meet these requirements.

The ship will make Hamburg in about one week, and the passengers will be forced to disembark.

Nations round the world were very conscious of the desperate situation for the refugees, but they all had problems of their own. Unemployment among their own populations loomed large, as did a shortage of housing. So most nations set a quota for the number of applicants they would take, and reckoned that though their combined total would certainly not solve the problem, their contribution would be better than nothing.

In Britain, there were all sorts of lower-level attempts to help out. The example below is typical.

Letters, W Joseph, Central Office for Refugees. May I, through your columns, appeal for the loan of one or more large empty houses in the Centre or West End of London, to be used as a hostel for German refugee women who are brought to this country by our Committee to take up posts as domestic servants.

These women often arrive in London in the evening and need a day or two, if not longer, before they can find or enter a post. Others already in the country need a similar refuge in between posts.

Such a hostel would serve not only for this purpose but could be used as a much-needed training centre for a limited number of women who wish to take up domestic service but who, although suitable in other ways, are ignorant of our language, customs, household equipment, etc, and for whom a period of a month's training or conditioning would be of inestimable value.

While my Committee can see its way to paying for the maintenance of such a hostel and training centre, it would not be easy to pay a commercial rent. We are, therefore, begging for one or more houses as near as possible to Bloomsbury House either to be let at a nominal rent or, better still, to be lent rent free. Any offers of this kind would be gratefully received.

AMERICAN INVOLVEMENT AT THIS TIME

The US could not quite make up its mind about the situation in Europe. Nearly every one was opposed to Hitler. The Fascism he espoused was diametrically opposed to their own capitalist system, and his dictatorship was contrary to their own democracy. And they were appalled by his habit of taking over his small neighbours.

At the same time, about half of them were most anxious that the US should not get into a war again. They preferred a splendid isolation, and thereby avoided being dragged into other people's conflicts. In fact, a few years earlier they had even passed a Neutrality Act that forbade their nation from supplying arms to anyone involved in a war, or to any likely combatant. At this time, this meant that the US would not provide the armaments that Britain badly wanted and was asking for.

President Roosevelt, apparently anxious to provide that assistance, gave a public address, once or twice a month, that hectored Hitler on the way he should behave, and ended with an empty bluff that he would soon be in trouble if he did not behave. Hitler replied with a mixture of derision and bravado, and said that there was no way he would change. It was good fun, at a schoolboy level.

There was also, in capitalist America, a section of the nation that was licking its lips at the thought of how much profit could be made by selling all sorts of arms and weapons if a war did break out. To them, though it was essential that the USA not get herself involved in the fighting. Profitable trade was all that mattered.

King George VI had just finished a very successful Royal Tour of America, in which he was immensely popular with the public, and he cemented the already strong bond between the two countries. When he returned to Britain, he was greeted with this notice below. It was presented in this most unusual full-page advert in *The Times*, with the compliments of the famous retail store Harrods, and you will notice that the writers were about as effusive as it is possible to be.

A Salute to
The Royal Ambassadors
Of Friendship

From a conquest without parallel in history, from a victory which has lifted the spirit and cheered the souls of half mankind, from the happiest crusade that the world has ever known, our King and Queen come smiling back to Homeland.

Not merely with loyal and dutiful greeting do our people receive them, but with a heightened pride and gratitude beyond all pageantry of welcome; for they have turned the eyes of a troubled world to brighter horizons, towards the vision splendid.

They have proved that the true nobility of character, inborn graciousness and selfless devotion contribute more surely to the goodwill and contentment of peoples than all the armories of earth.

God grant that one day this lesson will be learnt the wide world over that individuals and nations will come to build, here a little, there a little, on these foundations, enduring peace and happiness and freedom for all children of men.

God Save Their Majesties

OZ-WAR-TIME NEWS

The national register. The Australian Government had wisely decided that, when they brought down the Federal budget in about two months, more taxation would need to be collected. How they would do this was still a matter for argument, but one way was to introduce a new type of taxation that involved a person's wealth, as distinct from income. That would mean that any holding of assets might attract some form of taxation on it, at a percentage rate. Thus, any forms of property, shares, debentures, businesses, farms, cash in the bank, jewellery, motor cars, and the like, could attract this tax.

The trouble for the Government was that it had no idea of what assets people held. So, given that the 5-yearly national Census was coming up soon, it passed legislation that enabled it to include questions about every person's "wealth". These questions, called a **Wealth Survey**, were to be on a separate form, it was compulsory to answer them if you had total wealth in excess of 500 Pounds, and there were very substantial penalties, including fines and imprisonment, for not giving correct and complete responses to them. On top of this, there was a **Person Survey** that required men to give details of their name address, age and job.

Concerning **the Wealth Survey**, civil libertarians opposed it on the basis that it was an unnecessary invasion of the privacy of the individual. The man in the street agreed with them. But large numbers also objected because they had seen the Hitler Government do the same thing. In Germany, they had required all Jews to fill out such forms, and had then used them as the basis for simply taking away their assets. What was our Government up to? Could we be facing an assets grab in this country?

The second form roused the ire of the Trade Union movement. It considered, rightly, that the Government was compiling a **National Register** of men suitable for service in the armed forces, and that it would be used to impose conscription **for overseas service.** On top of that, the Unions said there was no place for **the conscientious objector** to register as such, so that his special need might be ignored in a general call-up.

The all-sweeping and threatening way in which the enabling Bill was worded added to this apprehension.

Letters, Kathleen Fitzpatrick. The Bill does not define the nature of the information which citizens must furnish. The form of registration attached to the Bill is rendered meaningless by Section 27 which gives the Government power to make regulations "prescribing all matters which by this Act are required or permitted to be prescribed or which are necessary or convenient to be prescribed."

Citizens are to be rendered liable to fine or imprisonment (Section 27) for failure to disclose information demanded by the Board, or by anyone to whom it may delegate all or any of its power. Such persons are given unlimited authority to make "enquiries and observations". These words appear to leave the way open for a regime of spying and searching which would certainly vitiate every democratic principle.

I can tell you that **it is now too late to protest**, because the legislation has already been passed. But it was passed without the support of the mass of the population, and was remembered and resented by many voters when they next went to the polls.

POST SCRIPT. The Menzies Government, after much harassment by the Trade Union movement, agreed to change the legislation to eliminate problems with **the Person Survey**. The **Wealth Survey** continued on unchanged.

PREPARING FOR WAR IN OZ

Now that Menzies was in the saddle as Prime Minister, what was happening to our national preparations for a possible war? Well, it seems that not everyone was going with hysterical suggestions of moving children from the cities to country regions.

This idea was floated because Britain had decided to do just that. Surely, if some similar war broke out here, Australia should follow the Mother Country.

Press clipping. Revaluation of plans for the evacuation of children from the cities **in a national emergency** (undefined) may be necessary, because of the disinclination of parents to agree to separation from their children.

Questionnaires asking parents to supply information regarding the number of their children and whether they would acquiesce in their evacuation to safe country districts have been distributed in the country areas.

It is believed that a majority of parents, while co-operating to the extent of supplying the information sought, will indicate that they would oppose children being taken from them and sent to the homes of strangers.

There is no compulsion about this section of the Victorian air raid precaution plans, the weakness of which is the probability that children evacuated from the city would be unable to return home immediately the emergency ended.

Officials of the Education Department said that they could not understand why any children should become frightened that war had broken out when they were given the questionnaire forms to be taken to their parents.

The word "war" did not appear on the form and the average child would be unable to place that interpretation on "national emergency" which was the designation used throughout the form.

Comment. Blind Freddie could have told them that parents would not let their children go to the homes of strangers at a time when parents were most needed. Granted, such a move was viable in Britain's big cities, but this was because they were so big. Here, every back yard had enough space for an air raid shelter that would give protection from everything except a direct hit. In any case, it seemed likely that air raids would occur in Britain in the immediate future, while **in Oz the possibility seemed remote for the present**.

In the last two paragraphs, it seems **the Education Department thought our kids were too dumb to realise that war was on the horizon**. Thank Heavens the Education Department was around to inject some common sense into matters.

ARE OUR MEN READY FOR~WAR?

Letters, STILL KEAN, Allambee. It is well known how the small town of Mirboo North responded to the recent militia recruiting campaign. Many promises were made, but full uniforms and equipment have not been issued, and some recruits of three month's standing have not even rifles. We are wearing our own clothes out with military work. Lack of uniforms keep us from attending ceremonial parades, to which we have had several invitations. Text-books, so necessary for our studies, are out of print and unobtainable.

Although started in February, we have not had a pay night yet, and are now told that there is little hope of receiving any pay or travelling allowance.

My case is one of many. I live 15 miles out of Mirboo north, and besides devoting much of my spare time to the work, I have attended 12 parades, involving a total of 360 miles in my own car, for which I am entitled to 12 Shillings, but have no prospect of receiving same nor pay for the work done. As for the bonus, ...?

INTRODUCTION OF NATIONAL SERVICE

News Item. The introduction of **universal military training for young men may be postponed** as an outcome of a survey of the three year's defence program which was begun today. The survey is needed for the upcoming budget.

In the course of this review, the Minister may consider changes in the programme.

The question of the re-introduction of universal military training is certain to be reviewed. Most members of the

Cabinet are strong supporters of universal training, and it is taken for granted that the Menzies Ministry will make it an ultimate objective.

Present indications are, **however**, that it will not be re-introduced before July, 1940, at the earliest, because of the shortage of equipment and educational staff. The Cabinet is also expected to review the decision to establish a mobile force. Several Ministers consider that the money spent on this force could be better used for universal training. It is possible that a decision may be reached to postpone action until the future of universal training is decided.

Comment. It seems that the Government's policies and planning were not well thought out, and were not being administered at all well. Perhaps they might improve if war came to our shores. At this stage, you would hope so.

PROBLEMS WITH YOUR CAR

The Argus started the ball rolling with an Editorial commenting on "road hogs" who were being fined at a record rate. From there, opinion and fact flowed freely.

Letters, ANTI-FLASHNESS. Undoubtedly many motorists who are fined for breaches of the traffic regulations are only hurt financially, and they regard this as "a cheap get-out". Why not, in addition to fining them, **impound the car for from seven days upwards**, according to the offence. The offender would then not only be out of pocket but would suffer the inconvenience of being deprived of his car.

Letters, JUSTICE. Instead of perhaps building a casualty hospital for the traffic victims, could not the man or woman causing an accident, through recklessness, be **given time in gaol**? This is done in New Zealand, with excellent results. What does the road-hog care for a fine or caution? Think of the horrible suffering to the victim, and the shock and suffering to relatives. The toll of the road could be stopped if offences were not treated leniently.

Letters, LESS SPEED. It seems extraordinary that in road accidents drivers who are convicted of carelessness should be let off with a fine of a few pounds. Why are they not punished in the same way as other miscreants – with some months in gaol with hard labour, **and the permanent loss of their licence?**

There should be a speed limit in towns and suburbs, as the excuse so often is "I swerved to avoid a dog." If the man had not been travelling at such speed he would have seen the dog in plenty of time to be able to avoid it or any other obstacle on the road without running into some person or post, as the case might be. As for drunken drivers, they should certainly get gaol when caught, and in a case in which some unfortunate citizen is killed **they should be liable to be hanged like any other murderer**, because they know that if they drive while "under the influence" they are liable to have accidents and cause deaths.

Letters, A NETTLEFOLD. I appreciate the problems of the City Council in its parking problem, but after seeing parking meters in use and their enormous expansion in America, I am certain they offer a solution. The parking meter means the marking off of sections, and the placing of a small coin by car owners in the meter, which then ticks off the time allowed, at the expiration of which the meter shows the car to be illegally parked, and punishment follows. Nothing could be more simple, and nothing more just than to pay for space provided.

Surely the council cannot stop the wheels of progress by prohibiting the parking of a man's car when he wishes for a brief period to call and transact business, especially when he is willing to pay a small fee for the time he occupies the space. Now we shall all be compelled to carry a driver, who during the period of our call will cruise around until our return, thus adding to the congestion.

Branding of drivers. There was a number of letters calling for **the branding of bad drivers**. This does not mean stamping their foreheads or putting a tattoo on their wrists. It meant putting something like a large sticker on their car, so a bad driver could be identified as such.

Letters, Marcus Wettenhall. I support the suggestion of Loftus Moran. I would suggest that every responsible motorist who would undertake the duty should be appointed an observer or honorary patrol officer. When registered he should be provided with a notebook setting out salient points of cases to report, such as car number, time, place, witness. This notebook would be his authority, and in more serious cases he should have a badge to display indicating assistance required. The restraining influence on all drivers of not knowing who was watching would be greater than any number of official police patrols.

If there were a few thousand observers on the way into and about the city every day the road hog would be reported three or four times. These reports would be independent corroborative evidence, and police could act appropriately.

Not everyone saw the need for these rangers. The Victorian Commissioner of police thought that reported results would be too "fragmentary" to be useful, and also that **the type of persons who would want to become rangers would be unbalanced, vindictive, and perhaps motivated by revenge**. The Chief Secretary thought the applicants would be just meddlesome busybodies, who would bring chaos into a system that was now working well.

In turn, not everyone agreed with **them**.

Letters, Let's Get Busy. While driving along the Beach Road at Elwood at 12.45 on Wednesday morning a motor-car passed me at a speed which could not have been less than 70 miles an hour. My own speed at the moment was 32 miles an hour, yet almost in a flash the maniacal drier of the other car had traversed a quarter of a mile of straight road and rounded a bend, taking him out of my sight.

The point that is perplexing me is this. If I had taken this road hog's number and reported the incident to the police in the hope that an official lecture, at least, would be administered, would I thereby have entered the class sneered at by the chief Secretary as "meddlesome busybodies"; or would I have done a duty to my fellow men by helping to discipline a cad whose presence on the road must always be a menace?

There were other ways to deter deviant drivers. Here we have a suggestion of the **most dastardly schemes** under official review.

News item. Mr Bailey said yesterday that the immediate effect of the introduction of **"on-the-spot" summonses** would probably be a marked increase in revenue from fines. It was reasonable however, to expect that they would have a salutary effect on road users, and eventually reduce traffic breaches. If adopted, the system would not be used exclusively against offending motorists. **Careless pedestrians and cyclists would be liable as well.**

Rejecting a suggestion by Mr Allnutt, MLA, that legislation should be introduced to **control the speed of motor-cars by fitting governors to cars**, the Premier (Mr Dunstan) said yesterday that more accidents were caused by total disregard of the rules of the road and the rights of other road users than by excessive speed. The best solution was more policing, more prosecutions and the cancellation of driving licences for serious breaches.

Mr H Allibon, Secretary of the Automobile Chamber of Commerce, said: "**I am heartily in favour of fitting governors**, and think they should add to it a provision that the proposed **traffic court should sit night and day.**"

When an offender is detected, he should, within the shortest possible time, present himself in that court. And if his offence is bad the penalty should be heavy. There was no reason why a motorist should be kept wondering whether he would be prosecuted. If a traffic officer was satisfied that he had committed an offence, the sooner the prosecution was heard, the better.

You will be pleased to know there was some opposition to these suggestions. For example, Mr Alfred Kelly, president of the Royal Automobile Club, said **"We emphatically oppose any suggestion of the on-the-spot fines."**

Comment. In case you hadn't noticed, let me tell you that on-the-spot fines **have** been introduced, and what great little revenue-raisers they are. I am not all that sure about what has happened to traffic.

KILLING KOALAS

Letters, Antipodean, Melbourne. May I point out that koalas are evidently being deliberately slaughtered by some persons, and their fur exported for trade purposes?

Just before Christmas, in London, there appeared in the Christmas catalogue of a world-famous Regent Street firm of men's outfitters an advertisement for motoring gloves backed and gauntleted with Australian native-bear fur – priced at 45 shillings a pair.

I went to the shop, saw the gloves, and found the description authentic beyond doubt. In answer to my inquiries, the salesman told me that since the publication of the Christmas catalogue, at least a dozen Australians in London had come on the same errand as myself.

Several had threatened to make a complaint to the Australia House authorities; if so, no action had as yet been taken. As I left England a few days later I was unable to find out if any steps were contemplated to prevent an indefinite continuance of the scandal.

JULY: HITLER'S NEXT VICTIM

By now, everyone was pretty sure that Poland would be the next victim of Hitler. For example, he was building up his troops on the border, and sometimes making little raids inside Poland's territory, "chasing miscreants" who had crossed into Germany. He was smuggling German officers into Poland posing as tourists, and their purpose was to organise and train Germans there for when they were needed. He was having on-again, off-again talks with Poland, and always making demands to get more German territory back, with Danzig at the top of his list. He accompanied these talks with utterances, in public or in private at the consular level, that he was ready, willing and able to crush Poland at any time. Poland, at the same time, was beating its chest and poking its tongue out, confident that the thought of war with Britain and France would deter Hitler from attacking.

Little did Poland know, what has since been revealed, that **on April 13th, Hitler announced that he would invade Poland on September 1st**, and ordered his military to start preparing for that date. As the months from April till July passed, he had not changed that date at all, and throughout that time, his Wehrmacht (military forces) made ready for that date. If Poland had been aware of this, I suspect she would have been taking her discussions with Germany much more seriously than she had up till then.

Hitler was now complaining that Britain and France were making treaties with all the nations on its borders, and was trying to "encircle her". Of course, he was completely right. England wanted to surround Germany with countries that would all stand up to and oppose him.

Letters, Peter Pendergrass, Oxford. I read with wonder of our ambassadorial efforts to encircle Germany. Of course, it is a great idea to do that. But we are not doing it properly. What we should have is agreements that **all** nations on Germany's boundaries will fall upon the dictator if he invades **any one** of them. Can you imagine his response if he was attacked by some eight nations, on eight fronts, at the same time.

But of course, I am away in the clouds. There is no chance of getting all of them to agree to do this. On the one hand, many of them are frightened of Germany. On the other hand, they have been fighting each other for centuries, and they hate each other. There is no chance they would join together even for something so sensible as this.

I am sure our diplomats know what is needed, and that there is no use in going for that. So, somehow they have to justify their existence, so instead they go for one-on-one treaties. A fat lot of good that will do everyone.

Germany really was in an encircled position. Before she took over Austria and the Czechs, there **were 10 countries on her border**, and another **six to the North within a stone's throw**. But look at it from Hitler's point of view. **All of that presented not a real threat, but rather the opportunity for further easy conquests.**

Look at Denmark and Luxembourg to the West. Both were small and militarily weak and just a drive over the border from Germany. If they were attacked by Hitler, it would be suicide to resist. Holland and Belgium, being a bit stronger, might fight back, or they might not, but their fate too would be suicide in the long run.

To the East was Poland. If Hitler was looking for a victim, this was a pretty good bet. No-one near her was likely to come to her aid, it was well known that her defences were back in the days of the cavalry, and not up there with the fast-moving tanks and planes of the Germans. Her army had less than half the German numbers. She would be easy pickings if a big bully like Germany pounced.

Letters, Stan McKillop, Glasgow. Suppose Hitler invaded Poland and we went to her rescue. Then how do we get troops and supplies to her. We can't take them across the neutral countries of Belgium and Holland, and Norway, and I can't imagine Germany would give us a welcome. We could send them by sea, up into the North Sea, and into the Baltic. I can't imagine we would slip unseen past Germany. Could we land them at Danzig, a Polish port already under Nazi control? Is our Air Force prepared to, and able, to bomb targets in Germany, and would that provoke retaliation from Germany? **I think our promises to help Poland are empty**, and we should stop promising help we cannot deliver.

OZ WORKERS OFF TO BRITAIN

News item. Nearly 80 skilled workshop employees, several professional officers of the Victorian, NSW, South Australian, and Queensland railways, and other skilled men from private engineering firms, would leave for England soon. They would be trained in the manufacture of airframes for Bristol Beaufort bombers,

To meet the requirements of the Bristol Aeroplane Company, the trainees had been divided into four parties, the first of which, consisting of 22 men and a supervisor, would leave for England on the *Mooltan* on July 23, the Minister for Supply (Mr Casey) said yesterday. The second, third, and fourth parties would leave at five-weekly intervals thereafter. The period of training in England would last for approximately 10 weeks, but would vary accordingly as circumstances changed.

Mr Casey said it was expected that all of the trainees would return to Australia before March 1, 1940. Establishment of the **aircraft industry in Australia** would provide employment at the peak of production for approximately 4,300 men, of whom 1,000 would be employed in Victoria, 1,000 in New South Wales, 1,800 in South Australia, and 500 in Queensland.

OZ IN ASIA

While everything seemed to be happening over in Europe, there was another conflict brewing on our own doorstep that we should keep an eye on. For the moment it was centred on China, where the Japanese had annexed a vast tract of wilderness land in the North West. They had occupied this land in 1937, called it Manchukuo, said it was an independent new State, and proceeded to extract its coal and minerals at a fast rate. China thought this was a funny way for a neighbour to act, and so the two nations made war.

A current Tokyo report pointed out that July 6th was the second anniversary of the start of their conflict. The day was marked by a military parade through Tokyo, and by fireworks at night in the major cities. It was estimated that **Japan now had 10 million troops spread throughout China, Mongolia, Manchukuo, and sundry islands**. China, on the other hand, had twice that number under arms, and was training lads and girls down to the age of 14 for military service. Japan now occupied one-sixteenth of China's land area, but that included over half her mainland ports.

Comment. This report went out of its way to present an anti-Japanese picture. It talked about grumbling among its citizens, inflation, the rise in national debt, friction in the army, and the poor treatment of men sent back from the front. However, "foreign observers agree that Japan can carry on for several years. Her population, if need be, can live on rice and fish. But whether the Japanese, who are one of the most servile people of all, will stand a further tightening of the belt seems open to doubt." It added that controlled newspapers give the public a false picture of the invincibility of the armed forces. Also, Japan was hoping that Britain would go to war with Germany so that she could demand a free hand in Asia as the price for her neutrality.

Further comment. At the moment, the British were involved in a serious situation at Tientsin in China. For about a century, Britain had had **a concession** there that allowed her to occupy a defined large part of the city and to use it as a base for trade with all of China. The Japanese, via their war with China, had occupied the Tientsin area, and were now harassing the British there. For example, they had blockaded the port against British ships, and molested male and female British subjects, and even killed a few. Right now, the two nations were in serious talks about the future of the concession, and indeed the future of British trade with China. At the same time, demonstrations and even riots against Britain were occurring in Japan proper, on a large scale, and anti-Britain feelings were being whipped up by a regime that argued that Britain should be doing more to help Japan in China.

This left Australia feeling very uneasy. So far, the anti-Britain feeling had not spilled over to Australia, but it was clearly on the cards. What was also of significance was that **Japan was thumbing its nose at Britain, and also America,** and was clearly almost ready to pit its arms against them, and us.

WARDENS HARD TO RECRUIT IN OZ

Mr P Robinson, the City of Melbourne Engineer, expressed disappointment at the response to the appeal last week for persons to apply for voluntary positions of Air Raid Wardens. He said it was apparently difficult to raise interest in or to get people to prepare for things that might never happen.

Only 108 applications were received, including 16 women. One applicant was a planter from Malaya, who was in Melbourne for only a few months, and who thought it proper that he should help out in an emergency while he was here.

Of course, volunteers for the position would have been the greatest pessimists in the world. In Britain, not a single bomb had fallen, and there was as yet not one shot fired.

So who needed wardens? In Australia, 12,000 miles away, it was hard to believe that we would need wardens even if all of Europe started to fight. So the few who volunteered at this stage must have expected the very worst to happen.

VICTORIA EXCITED BY A NEW GOVERNOR

Sir Winston and Lady Dugan will take up their new position this afternoon. They will berth at Melbourne's Prince's Pier at 8am, and the Premier, Mr Dunstan, will go aboard, and make a formal call. The new arrivals will disembark at 10am at the pier where a naval guard of honour will give a royal salute. Later, he will be sworn in as Governor at the Parliament House, and then proceed in state to the Domain, where a seventeen-gun salute will be sounded.

When the *Ulysses*, in which their Honours shipped, arrived in Adelaide a few days ago, they were greeted excitedly by Lady Dugan's terrier, Jimmie, who had come separately for quarantine reasons. When he heard her voice, he jumped wildly on the pier. Jimmie and several pet turtles will be taken to Melbourne after Lady Dugan has settled into her new home.

COCKTAIL PARTIES AT SEA

Sydney news item. Protests against the holding of **cocktail parties on warships** have been made to the Minister for Defence by Mr Collins, MHR. He said that such occasions might provide opportunities for spies to obtain information. "A ship of war is no place for such gatherings, particularly in these times," Mr Collins said. "Nowadays **spies are everywhere** and unfriendly people may be within our gates ready to sieze such opportunities for obtaining important information concerning our defences for the purpose of passing it into the hands of potential enemies. The practise is wrong, and should be stopped immediately.

Also, the ratings cannot be expected to feel happy with their lot when they witness crowds at cocktail parties aboard ships, while they are denied some little concession or privilege they may be seeking from authorities."

MYSTERIOUS MUTTERINGS ON ALIENS

A suggestion that some action might be taken within a few days to **counter** any attempt at Nazi and other **alien espionage** in Australia was made by the Federal Attorney-General (Billie Hughes) today. Mr Hughes refused to elaborate on this statement, which he made in reply to a question as to whether any steps were being taken to combat the activities of alien agents.

It is believed that the action forecast by Mr Hughes will be provision to enable a clearer check to be made on the movements of all aliens, particularly those who, like the Reich Germans, are organised in support of a political system opposed to democracy.

"The investigation branch of my department **is keeping a close watch on all suspects**," Mr Hughes said, "so that we may take what measures are necessary to counter any espionage. Some of the gentlemen concerned appear to assume that the Government will take no action, no matter what they do. They may find themselves mistaken. I would not be surprised to hear something within a few days."

It turned out that when the Germans and Italians did enter the War, the Government did have lists of aliens ready, and so **the citizens from those countries were interned without delay**.

INIQUITOUS BILLIARD ROOMS

Letters, Violet Lindrum, Goulburn. I am voicing the opinion of every billiard-room proprietor and player of the grand old game, in protesting most strongly against the recent statement by Commissioner of Police, McKay, who said that **if he had his way, all billiard rooms would be closed down**, because they exercise a harmful influence over the morals of youth.

Why, in the name of common sense, should billiard rooms be singled out as harmful? I am sure no proprietor wishes to see persons of doubtful character on his premises. Why not close racecourses and hotels as well? Victimisation has no place in a sane society. Neither has high-handed autocracy, and the sooner a little common sense is applied to the problems of governing this country, the better place it will be to live in.

A NATION GOING TO THE DOGS

If you want evidence of this, see the five items below.

The scourge of painted lips. This warning is given by the Bishop of Willochran (the Right Rev. Dr Richard Thomas) in a letter to his clergy which appears in the July issue of the diocesan paper.

From various sources, complaints have reached me about the objectionable practice, now, alas, becoming increasingly prevalent, of women and girls with painted lips presenting themselves at the altar rails for Holy Communion. It is obvious that this habit is open to serious objection when receiving the chalice, and is liable to cause painful distraction to the minds of devout communicants.

The growing habit of painting the face and the use of lipstick is much to be deplored, and feminine charm has considerably depreciated since its introduction. I desire that you, my reverend brethren, admonish your parishioners in respect to this matter and warn women and girls with painted lips not to present themselves for Holy Communion.

At the same time I consider that men should refrain from smoking before receiving their communion. This is an occasion for the exercise of Godly admonition, and I trust that you will make known my directions at a service in church and on other occasions as need shall arise.

Swing and pictures. Court judgement, Brisbane. In these days of super-civilisation, the **seven deadly sins** are stalking the nation and hatred and avarice are entering the spirit of our daily lives. So said Justice Brennan, in sentencing an 18-year old employee for taking 400 Pounds from the National Bank.

Justice Brennan said that the youth of today had to bear the brunt of unfortunate circumstances, and was looked on as cannon fodder for war, or to be thrown into discard. When a youth however obtained a chance of a good position in a bank and broke a law like this, an example should be made of him.

Mr Justice Brennan also remarked that youth was out to enjoy its privileges, namely **swing music and pictures.**

"But ask them to read a newspaper or if they know anything about what is happening in the world, well that is foreign to them."

Less swing at Uni. News item. Melbourne University students will not be allowed to spend their luncheon hour mastering the intricacies of the latest dance craze at organised recitals at the Union Theatre.

Students' apathy towards political and sociological meetings and their like have caused the Student Representative Council to impose restrictions on mid-day dances and music recitals. The various Swing groups will have to refrain from sponsoring recitals that might clash with those of the Fine Arts Society.

Slot machines must go. It was said officially today that all poker and other machines that may be operated as games of chance must be removed immediately from all clubs, including golf clubs, in New South Wales.

Police will visit the clubs, and clubs that have disobeyed the order will be prosecuted. Under the Gaming and Betting Act, police have the power to have declared as common gaming houses all club premises where the machines are being used.

Police allege that inquiries have revealed that poker and similar machines are being operated on the premises of most clubs in Sydney including golf clubs. Many of the machines are leased to the clubs by the importers on a 50-50 basis, and in the opinion of the police, the business in some cases has become a racket. Most of the machines have been imported from the United States.

It is said that in at least five premises in Sydney, thousands of the machines are in store, waiting to be leased or loaned on a basis that would return substantial revenue to the importers. Many of the machines, according to the police, are "doctored" so that the persons operating them have no chance of winning.

Popular games of chance. Proscription of skill-ball and certain other means of gambling as unlawful games has been suggested by the Victorian Commissioner of Police.

Mr Duncan proposes **that skill-ball, baccarat, minah dinah, chemin de fer, darto, and ringalet be brought under that Section of the Police Offences Act** which prohibits fan-tan, two-up, and other games of chance.

Mr Duncan has also suggested that legislation should be enacted to make it compulsory for the secretary of an agricultural society or similar body to obtain the approval of the police before issuing permits to individuals to operate "side shows" and other games at agricultural shows or similar assemblages.

AUGUST: RUSSIAN – GERMAN PACT

While Britain (and France) was running madly seeking treaties with everyone, Russia was more deliberately pursuing only two major ones. The first was with the British. It wanted the Brits to sign a non-aggression pact for 25 years, but the shallowness of the British response was more than testing its patience. For example, in mid-August, a British delegation arrived in Russia after a 5-day passenger boat trip, that could have flown there in a single day. The senior British official had come without proper credentials, so that his input had no validity. Further, when the Soviets offered 136 military divisions in a mutual defence against Germany, the British offered six. Surely, the Poms were not really serious.

Russia, however had another playmate. **She was also talking to Germany.** This was quite a surprise. After all, **from Russia's point of view, Germany was just one more capitalist oppressor.** From Germany's vantage point, **Russia was the dreaded menace of international Communism** that Hitler had been reviling for twenty years. But, in these strange times, here they were talking seriously to each other.

What Hitler wanted was a guarantee that he would **not have to fight a major war on his eastern front.** If Russia would stay away from any war there, he would have no problem with taking over Poland, because he thought that the British and French were bluffing. In any case, if they got belligerent, he was more than a match for them, so he thought and hoped.

Hitler of course was also at other negotiating tables and perhaps was trying to get hold of Poland without resort to invasion. But he had not forgotten that **he had ordered his armed forces to be ready for war on September 1ˢᵗ**, and he had in no way changed that order. So, the only treaty he really wanted to conclude was the one with Russia.

So, on August 19ᵗʰ, **he was very pleased to gleefully report that Germany and Russia had concluded a trade treaty.** Then, on August 23ʳᵈ, he went all the way, and proclaimed to an **astonished world** that the two nations now had a military treaty that would protect each of them from the military operations of the other. Hitler was now free to pursue his grand plans for the immediate conquest of Poland, and his ultimate expansion to the East.

Chamberlain, **shocked to the core**, said that this Moscow Pact had come as "a surprise of a very unpleasant character", but re-affirmed that Britain and France would fulfill their obligations to Poland if she were invaded. Poland, stirred at last to activity, concluded a new mutual assistance pact with Britain. Over the next few days, till the end of the month, diplomatic activity among European nations was frantic, but it remained to be seen whether a major conflagration would be avoided.

Remember Hitler, on April 13ʳᵈ, had set September 1ˢᵗ as the start date for invasion. Would he stick to it?

HITLER'S MESSAGE TO DALADIER

Below, in a letter to French Prime Minister, Daladier, on August 29ᵗʰ, he sounds uncompromising on Poland.

Everything that you write in your letter, Herr Daladier, I feel just as much as you. Perhaps we, as old front soldiers, can understand one another quite easily in many ways. I beg you, please, to understand this: that it is impossible for a nation of honour to renounce almost 2,000,000 people and to see them ill-treated at its own frontiers. I therefore raised a clear demand. Danzig and the Corridor must return to Germany.

I see no way of being able to persuade Poland, which shields itself from attack under the protection of its guarantees, **to accept a peaceful solution**. But I would despair of an honourable future for my people if, in such circumstances, we were not determined to solve the question in one way or another. If fate thus forces our two peoples once more fight one another, there will be this difference in our motives – **I will be fighting with my people for the reparation of an injustice, and you for its preservation**. This is all the more tragic in that many of the great men of your own people have recognized not only the senselessness of the solution originally laid down but also the impossibility of its continued preservation.

I fully realize the grave consequences which such a conflict produces, but I believe Poland would have to bear the gravest consequences, for no matter how a war about this issue ended, the present Polish State would be lost one way or another. That our two people shall enter into a new and bloody war of extermination over this question is very distressing, not only for you but for me, Herr Daladier. But, as already mentioned, I see, so far as we are concerned, no possibility of being able to bring any influence to bear on Poland to make her adopt a reasonable attitude so as to correct a situation which is unbearable for the German people and the German Reich.

DALADIER'S REPLY

At an hour when you speak of the gravest responsibility of shedding the blood of two great peoples who long only for peace and work, I owe it to you personally and to our two peoples to say that the fate of peace still rests in your hands.

Up to this very day there exists nothing that need prevent a peaceful solution of the international crisis in honour and dignity for all people, **provided the same will to peace exists on all sides**. Together with the good will of France, I express that of all its allies. I can assure you, with the best conscience, that among the differences of view between Germany and Poland which have arisen with regard to the Danzig question, there is none that could not be submitted to such a procedure for the purpose of a peaceful and joint solution.

In such a grave hour, I sincerely believe that **no man of noble sentiments could want a war of destruction** to be undertaken without a last attempt at a peaceful solution between Germany and Poland. Your will for peace could work for this with all determination without infringing in any way the German honour.

HOW BRITAIN REACTED

Chamberlain voiced Britain's determination never to make concessions again. Parliament was immediately recalled, and passed **The Emergency Act**, that gave it power to secure the public safety, the defence of the realm, the maintenance of public order, and the prosecution of war. The aim was to ensure "the whole strength as well as the undivided purpose of the nation may be controlled and directed to the achievement of maximum results." However, to maintain the essential character of a democracy, Parliament would retain its ultimate authority.

To the German man in the street, there was no doubt that Britain would back down again. The Russian Pact was greeted as a **masterpiece of German diplomacy,** and would mean that Britain and France would henceforth be forced to stop meddling in purely German matters. They would go back to their Empires, and leave Germany a free hand in Europe. They certainly would not go to war.

To the British man in the street, there was no doubt that war was inevitable. Neither Britain nor Germany would retreat, and it was a great consolation that **Britain was in a far better condition for a war than she had been at the time of Munich**.

So, there was a frenzy of activity. For example, gold in large quantities was transferred from its traditional storage places to hush-hush vaults, perhaps somewhere in Wales. Art works were stripped from Public Galleries, and also went into secret locations. Stained glass in cathedrals was removed from lead-light windows and stored. Unemployed Jewish refugees were used as volunteers to fill sandbags around hospitals. Traffic key-points were painted with white stripes to make them more visible during blackouts. The attitude was **that no one wanted a war, but it has** hung over us for a year. Let's get on with it and get it all over.

BUT AMONGST IT ALL: Press report. The first day's play in the cricket game between England and West Indies at the Oval was entirely suitable to a three-day Test Match. The sun shone, the grass was pleasantly green, there was a crowd of 20,000 or so and, above all, there was a happy spirit which softened the austerity often experienced in a Test Match against Australia.

England's score is not a large one, but it was gathered pleasantly against bowling and fielding which were certainly worthy of the occasion, and if the last four wickets did fall for the addition of only 19 runs, well, that at least helped the game along. .....Oldfield's innings was of interest. He has all the appearance of a batsman who understands how to play good bowling, and he has the strokes to play deliberately and without fuss which demand a careful and attentive distribution of the field on the off-side.

Hardstaff, with the ball coming on to the bat at a good pace, was in his best and most charming mood. There is no batsman in the country who can drive the ball to the off-side of the wicket with a greater ease or grace........

WAR MOVES IN OZ

In the early part of August, the Menzies Cabinet made two important decisions. **Firstly**, they decided not to go ahead with the formation of the mobile force of some 12,000 men. They realised, as they should, that such a force was useless against the vast armies that were being employed in Europe, and that would certainly be used here and in Asia. Forget it.

The second was interesting. Menzies said that at times **nasho** was a necessary precaution, and it was wise to implement it. But **now** was not that time. He pointed out that the cost of doing it was great, and if it turned out that it was not necessary in the long-run, then it was all money wasted. Thus, the scheme for universal training of 21-year old youths **was now rejected.** He might need to re-think that later.

MENZIES AND THE RUSSIAN-GERMAN PACT

No sooner had he thus spoken than the signing of the Pact was announced. In the nation's headlines, **BOMBSHELL** was the most frequently used word. The second most common description was **THUNDER STRUCK.** Menzies, for the first few days, could only muster a handful of trite platitudes, saying that there were still hopes for peace, that negotiations were still proceeding, and that we must ignore dooms-dayers, and remain calm. Incidentally, nothing gets me closer to panic that someone telling me to stay calm.

Then, however, he made a great recovery. He, and Cabinet, with the backing of the Federal Public Service that must have been working long and hard, brought down a set of regulations that **shook the foundations of our society**. Up till now, we might have thought that Government was intrusive and heavy-handed. **Hereafter we got a taste of the real dictatorial State.**

The regulations included the following:

The Government may impose a curfew on any area, in which the population must remain indoors; it may prohibit the use of unofficial uniforms; it may ban processions and meeting; it may prohibit the emission of any form of light at night, and it may prohibit the conduct of any activities which might, by the emission of flames, convey information useful to the enemy. **Camp fires were out.**

It could control all aspects of air and sea navigation, public order, and the manufacture and marketing and pricing of goods. It could take over any wireless, cable, or other such equipment, it could at will examine articles arriving and leaving by post, regulate photography and where it could be used, and prohibit the making of meteorological observations or records likely to be useful to the enemy. It forbad the importation or possession without authority of pigeons. **Pigeon pies are out.**

Aliens must report change of address, they may be restricted to live in specified areas, and they may be interned. Hotel-keepers must keep a separate register of all alien details, including when and how they arrived in the country and when they expect to leave. Provision is also made to control the employment of aliens. **Aunt Sophia from Europe had better cancel that trip.**

For the duration of this legislation, passports will be issued for specific trips only, and prior authority of the Minister is required to get that passport. Ministerial consent is required for the hiring of any Australian aircraft for any purpose. **The Fiji holiday also gone.**

These regulations are only **a small sample** of those imposed. They were in documents of 60 pages, and covered so many aspects of life that it took weeks for these consequences to sink in. Note though, that when it was said applicants should apply for **Ministerial** approval, there was no hope at all of getting that approval. It would have saved a lot of wasted time if they had said straight-out that the matter was totally forbidden.

Regardless of what happened in Europe over the next few weeks, Australia was on a semi-war footing. It still had many other ways in which it could respond, for example, calling **all** of its men into the armed services, and perhaps implementing rationing, and so on. But this set of regulations was a big change for everyone. They introduced **the concept that Government does indeed control every aspect of our lives**, and further, that **this time, unlike WWI, a war could involve invasion of our shores,** and that we had better get ready for that.

JAPANESE RESPONSE

Before the Pact was announced, Japan and Britain were getting themselves into a very serious situation. Japan, battling hard in China, had occupied the mountains round the island of Hong Kong, and was moving resolutely towards there. Britain had held Hong Kong as a colony for 100 years, and felt so threatened by the Japanese advances that it had that day blown up all the bridges connecting the island to the mainland. At the same time, anti-British riots were almost daily events in Tokyo, and the animosity emanating from there knew no end.

The Russo-German Pact put a stop to this, at least for the time being. Japan was appalled by the Pact. It meant that Russia was now freed up on its western front, and could start to fulfill its ambitions in the east, where Japan had its own ambitions. On top of that, it was shocked that its German friend would get into bed with the leading Communist nation in the world.

So the Pact threw the Japanese Cabinet into such turmoil that it resigned a couple of days later. For the next few days, until the end of August, the Japanese Government was in chaos and a new Cabinet was still working out what it stood for. In the meantime, though, **early signs were that it would adopt a more conciliatory attitude towards its disputes with Britain. It remains to be seen if that stance continued.**

THE LEAGUE OF NATIONS

The League of Nations had been set up after WWI to provide services that would **reduce conflicts between nations**. Over the last decade, it had lost much of its potential,and now, in the face of likely European-wide violence, it was nowhere to be seen.

Letters, C Lewis. The League of Nations does not appear to have entered into any of the Press reports regarding the crisis: Italy, Germany, and Japan have all withdrawn from the League when its policy was found to be not in accordance with theirs. Soviet Russia, who loudly acclaimed the principle of the League, did not see fit to bring before the League its non-aggression pact with Germany.

The League is dead, and should be decently buried. We Australians should refuse to pay any of our hard-earned tax money for the burying of the corpse. Let us recall Lord Beaverbrook and Lord Rothermere's campaign for a self-supporting British Empire as one unit, in other words, a League of Nations within the Empire.

Comment. This point was well made. Throughout the newspapers of this time, there were virtually no references to the League. It was a completely spent force.

APPEAL TO HITLER"S GOOD SIDE

Letters, Amy Lewis. Hitler loves children. Would it be possible for the mothers' clubs, the women in charge of all children's institutions, welfare, kindergartens, crippled hospitals, etc, to send a combined cable message from Australia, New Zealand, England, France, and America, to Hitler to avoid the awful slaughter of millions of innocent kiddies? It may touch his heart which the best brains of man have been unable to do so far.

Comment. Yeah. Right.

JAPAN GETTING MORE COMMENT

Letters, H Gardener After reading last Saturday's overseas news, Britishers might be deluded with the hope that Japan, in view of the recent Hitler-Stalin understanding, will "swing over" to the side of Britain and France. The Russians can concede the Japanese no points in diplomatic astuteness. It would be unwise for Australians to entertain the belief that Japan is disposed to alter her far-reaching imperialistic and pan-Western Pacific aims. British interests are the principal "block" to Japan's attaining her ultimate objectives, which extend to Australia and New Zealand.

Japan might, of set purpose, appear less aggressive, with the hope that Britain will more confidently go to war with the axis Powers in support of Poland. Nothing would suit Japan's book better than for England to be embroiled in war with Germany, and thus have her hands full in Europe.

CARS IN AUSTRALIA

This nation had 800,000 motor vehicles. That means that (in round figures) about one **vehicle** for every ten persons. That is, about one in 15 persons owned a **car**. Or put it this way, about one **family** in 3 had a car.

Australia had more old cars (over eight years old) than any other country. Our proportion was 55%, America's was 35%, and Britain's was 10%.

SLAVERY IN ITS VARIOUS FORMS

It was our boast that the British Empire had swept slavery from the world, but slavery in many forms was still in existence or coming back to the world, said the Rev R Wilson Macaulay at Wesley Church yesterday.

Was it not slavery to be **confined in a concentration camp**, without trial, without hope, and under torture? That was worse slavery than anything the old Roman Empire knew. Men like Pastor Niemoller were kept in concentration camps because they would not stop preaching Christ in Germany. There was the economic slavery of men who were not free to work at the kind of employment for which they were born, who **had dead-end jobs or no jobs at all,** or whose only hope was the old-age pension, Mr Macaulay added. **His remarks were pointed at the Jews being kept in German concentration camps.**

There was another kind of slavery, he said. When the United States Senate held a commission into the workings of the armament ring, its findings were so astounding that, at the request of Great Britain and European Governments, they were not published. **Armament firms** would bring a type of slavery which would mean **enormous profits for a few concerns**, while the rest of the world went down in flames and ruin.

Comment. This armament ring was to become a major talking point later in the War. The US came under criticism, until it entered the War two years after it started, for making a fortune out of selling armaments to many different parties.

NO GREAT RUSH FOR TOP HATS

Melbourne's spring social season will be given an unprecedented boost in November by the arrival of the Duke of Kent. Men's outfitters are already preparing **stocks of formal wear of the latest English fashions** – new waistcoats, morning coats, lounge suits of English cut, striped trousers, and silk top hats.

Outfitters, however, do not consider that the "formal fashion boom" will approach that of the Centenary year, when as many as 20 top hats – a year's sale for most hatters – were sold in a week. The demand is not expected to be much greater than that which precedes Melbourne Cup week.

In the opinion of one outfitter, Melbourne will not make any serious effort to "ape London fashions" during the presence of the Duke and Duchess. "Most of the persons who will wear such apparel already have it in their wardrobes," he added. "There is a slightly increased demand for top hats, but otherwise demand is negligible. Most of the top hats, frock coats, striped trousers, etc, are either in boxes, surrounded by moth balls, or in theatrical wardrobes." He added that there would be a trend towards "London-cut" in ordinary tailoring, with a slightly higher waistline, bold stripe effects, and a fuller cut in both coats and trousers. The popularity of the black Homburg hat, worn with longer hair, was increasing.

WE DON'T WANT AUSSIE BOOKS

Australians do not want Australian books, or books about the Australian scene, Mr John Wallace, the author of a number of mystery novels, believes.

Mr Wallace said that during a recent tour of the East Coast, he had visited hundreds of libraries, and had found everywhere the same reaction.

"When a subscriber opens a book and finds it is about Australia, he snaps it shut and slips it back on the shelf. They don't want Australian, they want overseas, or imaginary, backgrounds. Libraries say they cannot afford to stock books which are not popular, so Australian authors have difficulty in becoming popular unless they assume the character of foreigners. I myself have now taken to writing my mysteries with English backgrounds, and they are selling really well since I changed."

SEPTEMBER: INVASION OF POLAND

At 4.45am, just before dawn, **on September 1st**, the German cruiser, *Schleswig-Holstein*, started shelling a Polish military depot in Danzig harbour. **At the same time, over a million troops, along with massive numbers of tanks, and supported by ferocious artillery fire, marched across the border from Germany into Poland.** Within a few hours, other forces from East Prussia and Slovakia joined the invasion, so Poland was under attack from three directions at once. Over the next few days, along the borders, **Polish cavalrymen carrying long lances were fully routed by German tanks and Stucka dive-bombers,** and the Polish Air Force was virtually destroyed.

Britain (and France), when confronted with this invasion, tried a number of diplomatic moves to retrieve the situation, but to no avail. Finally, at 11.15am, **on September 3rd**, Neville Chamberlain took to the air waves, and formally declared that **England was now at war with Germany. Australia followed suit immediately.**

IMMEDIATE EFFECT ON CIVILIANS

Strangely enough, this announcement came as something of a relief to the population of Britain. After all, it had lived, for over a year, with the day-in and day-out fear that war was likely. To hear that it was here at last filled people with dread, but at the same time they welcomed the prospect that something would be done to dispel the uncertainty and worry and fear.

The British Government flashed into action. It announced that military training was now compulsory for **all men, aged 18 to 41, except for those in reserved industries.**

It moved to round up 500,000 children of school age in cities and send them to the country, where they might be safe from the bombing raids. This was a massive task that was expected to be completed in a few days. Also, still assuming that bombs would be dropped on the cities, they closed venues where casualties would occur en masse. All theatres, whether live or movie, were shut. The Australian Rugby Union team, which had just arrived for a tour of Britain, was told to go home. Large meetings and demonstrations and parades were all banned.

At the same time, "**a complete blackout of the whole kingdom from sunset to sunrise** is decreed, and having effect for each night for the future." "Henceforth, the sounding of factory sirens and hooters is prohibited, except to give warnings of air raids." All telephone services with overseas countries were cut. **Gas masks were issued to all citizens who did not already have them.** All men in the military Reserves were called up for service forthwith.

Scotland Yard issued a "list of the routes along which people who wish to leave London by road may proceed as rapidly as possible. There are nine such routes. They will be operated as one-way streets in an outward direction from 7am today. Drivers coming into London are warned that they must keep clear of the selected one-way routes for evacuation."

There were many other regulations and Acts introduced. For example, how did insurance policies for damage and destruction of property work in time of war? What limits were placed on ARP Officers to stop them from arbitrarily requisitioning vehicles? When a vehicle was requisitioned, what compensation was payable? Such questions needed answers, and they were provided over the next few weeks. At the same time, rationing of petrol, via coupons, was introduced.

MILITARY ACTION IN POLAND

When Hitler said a few months earlier ago that the invasion would begin on September 1st, he told his military officers to be ready. The German Navy responded to this by moving its fighting fleet to the Mediterranean and Atlantic, as well as the North and Baltic Seas, and even to the Pacific. When war was declared, they were then ready to sink British vessels and merchant ships that were scattered all over the oceans of the`world.

Hitler's submarine Commanders had also got into position. So, on September 5th, the first casualties of the War were inflicted when a German U-boat torpedoed and **sank a passenger liner,** *Athenia,* on its way to Montreal. Of the 1,400 on board, 300 were Americans. Many persons were rescued by other ships, but about 250 persons drowned.

This sinking came as a great shock to England. Three days had gone past without air-raids, and despite all the precautions, people were starting to ask "What War?" **But not now.** This episode brought home to everyone that this war was serious. The dreaded Hun really was the **dreaded** Hun, no mistake.

THE BATTLE FOR POLAND

In the meantime, the Germans had established a number of breaches of the Polish lines, and were making steady progress eastwards. Their superiority in the air was devastating and left the valiant Poles unsupported on the ground. Hitler's **blitzkrieg** of lightning forward-drives with no stopping or settling in **was a completely new way of warfare**, and the Poles were without answer.

By September 17, the Germans occupied half the nation. On that day, the Russians predictably entered the fray, and attacked Poland from the west. Caught between the two huge armies, the Government of Poland, and a million Polish troops, retreated into neutral Romania , and Poland was lost. Pockets of resistance, mainly in Warsaw, held out till September 29th, but by then victory was undisputed, and **Hitler led a triumphant procession through the streets of that capital**.

Poland had fallen, all neatly done within one month. England and France had done virtually nothing to help them out. **Poland as a separate State ceased to exist.**

Long before these hostilities, France had built a defensive wall along the Rhine from Switzerland in the South, up to about the top of Holland in the North. This was a more-or-less continuous Line of fortifications that faced towards Germany, and they claimed that no armed force could get through it. This was called the Maginot Line. In the spirit of friendship, Germany had built a similar line, facing France, that was called the Seigfried Line, and was 400 miles long with 18,000 bunkers, and also tunnels and tank traps. These Lines were roughly parallel, and were about 20 to 50 miles apart.

Each Line itself was 20 to 40 miles wide, with every sort of armament bristling from it. When war was declared in

September, France started to advance from its Line forward and threatened the opposing Line of the Germans.

Sometimes they gained perhaps 10 to 20 miles, and the Press in the West was very jubilant, But often they lost out in battle, and the Press got all evasive and reported the "shooting down of 8 enemy planes on a day of fierce bombing and fighting."

Towards the end of September, British troops joined the French, and now were in position to join the attacks. But these attacks were of little value in the long run, and the best that can be argued is that they did draw a number of **German troops to the west when they might have otherwise gone to Poland.**

By the end of September, the two Lines had settled down, and the soldiers spent a boring five months waiting for something to happen. Given that an offensive war in Winter in Europe is extremely difficult, the chance of any action got less as the year gradually expired.

At the end of September in Britain, German U-boats were sinking too many merchant and naval ships. The Air Force was bombing some strategic targets in North Germany, but was losing too many bombers, and was wondering why. The Army, quickly increasing in size, was bedded down in the Maginot Line, and similar places.

On the other hand, the British population was not being bombed, and was gradually relaxing, just a little. **Maybe this war might not be so bad, after all.**

OZ MILITARY MATTERS

The Australian Army at the moment was built round a smallish number of Regulars. These were mostly soldiers and officers who had fought in WWI and who had stayed in service after the war ended. This group had been there for 20 years, they were full-time soldiers, and provided the stability and continuity that was needed for military planning and functioning. It also necessarily provided the Top Brass for the Army, and was quite jealous of its much vaunted position.

The new recruits were a different group altogether. Firstly, there were the 70,000 part-time reservists, recruits registered in the last few months. They were to be part-time soldiers, getting perhaps four weeks of initial training and then annual camps and weekly parades.

Now, however, the Government announced a set of measures in late September that allowed for men over 18 and under 41 to join the Regular Army as full-time troops, but **still protected from serving overseas**. One month earlier, there was no prospect that such a recruitment campaign would be worth the effort. Since then, it seemed that things had changed, with the war-time situation in Europe, and now young men were clamouring for a chance to serve. We will wait to see how many turn up and pass the various tests.

It was not that everyone was eligible. Men had to pass a fitness test. And an age test, not too young and not too old. And they had to be **not** working in certain **protected industries**. In the initial list of protected industries, there were 117 entries. This list would be expanded soon.

ENEMY ALIENS ARRESTED

Press report. Moving swiftly in the early hours of this morning, police patrols working under the direction of the Military Intelligence Service rounded up a large number of **enemy aliens** in Sydney and other centres in Australia.

The plans had been carefully organised, and the police made their arrests in accordance with lists of wanted men and women, based on the secret dossiers in possession of the authorities. The persons apprehended were taken to selected police stations, and spent the night in cells. Subsequently they will be **interned in prisons in country centres round the nation**. The movements of wanted persons had been carefully checked for some time before the orders were given for the round-up.

Moving scenes were witnessed in the darkness and early dawn, as men were ordered to leave their families and accompany the police. The internees themselves reacted in accordance with their various temperaments – some with blustering indignation, some with sullen acquiescence, and some with apparent resignation to one of the inevitable consequences of war.

In several cases, wanted persons were in possession of revolvers. The police themselves were armed to guard against any contingency that might arise. Large sums of money – in one case about 500 Pounds – were found in the effects of a number of those arrested.

The persons wanted were permitted to dress and say farewell to their relatives, but were kept continuously under police supervision. The raids were the culmination of many months of carefully co-ordinated effort between the military organisation and the State police, as well as the Federal authorities. Prominent Nazis have been kept under secret surveillance in a manner which enabled the lists of wanted persons to be revised and added to from day to day. Details of preparations for the round-up were so worked out that the motor transport fleet, manned and ready to move off at a minute's notice, was standing by not only throughout Sunday night, but also all Saturday night. The organization functioned with impressive smoothness.

The people of Australia would be amazed and gratified, an authority said tonight, if they could know the full history of this thorough and dramatic action for the protection of Australia against enemy activity within our borders.

Comment. I am not at all sure that OZ people **were** gratified by all this. The blatant propaganda report above fills me with horror as I write. This is Nazi Germany stuff, descending on people in the middle of the night and ripping them apart from their families. You can guarantee that the list of names they were working from was vastly exaggerated and created to glorify the agency that was backing it. In fact, over the next months, **large numbers of interned people were freed by our various courts.** But with war-time secrecy already in place in Oz by this time, no figures of how many people were taken, and how many were released, were available.

Comment. My grandfather was dragged out of his bed and interned for three years. He had served in the Australian Army in WWI, and had lived in this country for thirty years. But he was Italian. So off to the camp he went.

MR MENZIES GOES TO CHURCH

On Sunday, September 17th, Mr Menzies spoke at Scots Church, Melbourne. He said that "we will win the war. We have a strange, and, as the foreigner might say, a provocative belief in ourselves. It never occurs to us that we might lose, and I see no reason why it should. We believe that the truth is mighty and must prevail. That gives us this feeling that we will see this thing through and win.

"It is simple for a nation to lose its fine ideals during war and allow itself to be swallowed up in vapours that must lead to a feeling of revenge and injustice that sowed the dragon's tooth of war. Our purpose in war must be to prepare for a just and lasting peace."

These were fine sentiments, honestly presented, and were doubtless well received inside the august Church he attended. But there were plenty of others who were not so sanguine about forgiveness, and had a few words to say about that.

Letters, VWP. To begin a war, which experts predict will last probably three years at least, with talk about a just peace seems extraordinary. It will be accepted that many Germans do not wish to again experience all the horrors of war. Of course not; what nation would?

But as a nation they are behind Hitler. When on a recent visit to the other side of the world, I found that most of the Germans I met were 100 per cent supporters of Hitler. This is the second world war within 25 years created by Germany. Surely, that should convince the world of the mentality of the nation responsible, and for the need, when the time arrives, for a peace that will protect the generations to come. We have unforgettable records of the diabolical treatment of anyone who opposed Germany in the last war. We know that since then thousands of their own decent citizens have ended their lives up against a wall, their greatest crime being their inability to see eye to eye with the Hitler regime. We know how Germany brutally robbed and turned the Jews out of their country. Let all civilised countries say that these things must never happen again.

Mr Menzies came into more oblique criticism below.

Letters, ANZAC. I was in the Parliamentary gallery at Canberra listening to the Prime Minister making a statement. "We are at war," he said, "and the Government is doing everything in its power to help the Motherland. We realise that the fate of Australia, as a free nation is at stake, and that the will to win our way through to victory is not enough: we must also quickly help with the power to win.

"To that end we have called for volunteers for service at home or abroad wherever they can be of most use. We have already completed the formation of the 1st Division, and others will follow as quickly as is possible, so that the whole of our available manpower will be ready and prepared for any emergency. As soon as the volunteers sign their forms they are medically examined, and then drafted into the various units. The staff consisting mostly of AIF veterans, with a practical knowledge of all details concerning the encampment of large bodies of troops, has now completed the establishment in camp of the 1ˢᵗ Division. We are necessarily short of uniforms, equipment, and arms, but these are taking priority in all factories, and will quickly overtake the demand for them. In the meantime the training of the troops continues in a most satisfactory manner. An officer of high rank and proved ability has been appointed Commander-in-chief of all troops in Australia. This is just a brief summary of what we are doing, and to show that the Ministry is fully alive to the seriousness of the position."

The Prime Minister sat down amid ringing cheers – and **as he did so I reached and stopped the ringing. The alarm clock had awakened me from my dream and I remembered that we still had Mr Menzies and a Cabinet of politicians.**

PLONK FOR OUR TROOPS?

Letters, Reason. No doubt the issue of a daily ration of wine to members of the AIF would benefit makers and vendors of that commodity, but in proportion to the quantity and alcoholic content of the wine so issued it would be a menace to the physical and mental efficiency of the men who drank it. Experience confirms the verdict of science that alcohol is the enemy of muscular energy and endurance. **When strenuous effort is required the first to fall are the drinkers of alcohol.**

In one hard campaign a British general testified that the alcoholics dropped out first, and with such regularity as if they had been labeled. As France has been quoted, consider an extract from a report drafted by Professor Debove, of the Faculty of

Medicine, and Dr Faisano, of the principal general hospital of Paris, both Frenchmen. "It is an error to state that alcohol...gives energy for work or that it renews strength. The artificial excitement which it produces quickly gives place to nervous depression and weakness; in truth, alcohol is useful to nobody; it is harmful to all...." When the terrible necessity arises to train men for war, the objective must be their utmost efficiency.

NO STOCKING UP ON STOCKINGS

Letters, ELSTER. As your correspondent, Mr Nathan, points out, women have now an opportunity of proving their patriotism by refusing to purchase stockings, etc, made from imported silk. They could, if they would, (1) keep the money that would otherwise be sent abroad to a foreign country in their own country (and it will be needed before this war is over); and (2) vitally help Australia's principal industry, i.e. woolgrowing.

SAVE YOUR TOBACCO TINS

Letters, John Satchell. I feel compelled to direct attention to the absolute waste of tobacco tins. As a smoker of well over 50 years, I look back to the days when we could get the best of tobacco for the pipe 4oz at 1/3. What does one get now, a 2oz tin for 2/-? What of the tin? Is it to be cast away in a time like this? I say no.

Would this waste occur in Germany or Japan? It is time something was done to stop it. One company takes the tin back already.

A NEW SHOW FEATURE

A Highland pipe band contest in two parts, by city and country bands, will be a new feature at the Royal Melbourne Show this year. The first prize band in each division will receive a cup from the RAS, and there will also be first and second cash prizes in each division. The city bands that have already notified their intention of competing will be from the Victorian Police, Hawthorn, and Toorak, while the country bands are Ballarat, Geelong, Horsham, and Werribee and elsewhere.

The contest will be conducted by, and under the rules of the Victorian Highland Association, and will comprise a test piece and a quickstep. Pipe-Major Peter Stuart will judge the music, and a judge will be appointed to judge the contest. A massed demonstration of the 11 bands, supported by a large party of Highland dancers, will be held in the arena at 9 pm on the last Saturday of the Show. Highland dancing will also be held on the last Saturday of the Show on the Jersey Lawns.

LEADING DOG JUDGE

Mr Tom Thomas, one of the world's foremost dog judges, who is to make the awards in the Royal Show record entry of 1000 dogs, arrived in Oz from the US on Monday. Mr Thomas adjudicated at the Montreal show in 1937, and he has forfeited 20 judging appointments in Canada and the US to visit here.

THE MAN WHO MIGHT COME TO DINNER

The *Argus* conducted a poll of readers. Who would you like to have dinner with? The results were:

Adolf Hitler

George Bernard Shaw

Franklin Roosevelt

Benito Mussolini

Winston Churchill

Neville Chamberlain

Mahatma Ghandi

Madame Chiang Kai-Shek

The Duchess of Windsor

Gracie Fields

Comment.   What an uninteresting lot we Aussies were. If we made such a list now, would we still have no Aussies on it?   Would they all be sportsmen? Or, lord help us, American celebrities?

OCTOBER: THE BALTIC STATES ARE NEXT

Most of the action had now finished on the Eastern front. With the Poles fully routed, Germany and Russia divided up the spoils. This process went remarkably smoothly, among these two new friends, so that Germany got the eastern two-thirds of Poland, and Russia took the western third. **Poland disappeared off the face of the map.**

But Russia was not finished. Remember those three Baltic States we mentioned earlier. **Latvia, Lithuania and Estonia were now ripe for plucking**. For these three countries, Russia was able to "persuade" them that it was in their interest to become friends. For example, on October 17th, a Russian battleship and 10 other navy vessels visited Estonia, and displayed their considerable military might. They all entered into trade agreements with Russia, and at that same time, opened up a few major ports and other strategic areas to Russian occupation and control. Basically, **this meant that Soviet troops had the run of these countries**, but there was none of the devastation that resistance and war would have entailed. These takeovers by Russia were gradual, and went on for months and, after that, **lasted until the fall of Communism fifty years later**.

PROPAGANDA AND CENSORSHIP

Letters, Peter Wright, Cambridge. On September 29, the Air Ministry issued the following announcement: "Units of the RAF today carried out attacks on ships of the German Fleet ... **Some of our aircraft** have not yet returned." The German High Command was more forthcoming. It said that, of six British attacking aeroplanes, **five**

were shot down. Our own Ministry of Information **deigns neither to confirm** nor to contradict this report.

Then on October 1, the German High Command **claimed** to have brought down two French and 10 British planes over the Western Front. This enemy statement was given in the British radio news bulletin – again without official comment.

If the Ministry of Information **continues to refuse to give information or to comment** upon German official statements, we British will be forced into the unfortunate position of having to **believe these depressing and probably false German statements**.

Letters, Mary Hornyold-Strickland, Sizergh Lodge, Kendal. Why must the BBC condemn us to such deplorable transmission from our home station while the German and other foreign stations can still be heard so easily and clearly?

Why did the BBC tonight inflict us with so much of Herr Hess's speech with no suitable antidote for foreign listeners who must be puzzled at such publicity being given to unimportant enemy utterances?

And why did the BBC broadcast the enemy version of our losses in today's air battle without an official statement from our own authorities, confirming or denying the enemy's claims?

NOTE ON THE WESTERN FRONT

In the north, the French were still trying to break through the Siegfried Line into the Saar Valley, but were not going anywhere really. Further south, things were quite relaxed, with no sign of hostility between opposing armies, and indeed a degree of bon homie showing at times. As signs of winter became more obvious, it was clear that neither army would venture out into the cold, so it looked as though all would be quiet on the western front.

In England, those dreaded bombs had not fallen, apart from some on naval bases in Scotland. It was starting to look as though Hitler would keep his promise of not bombing English cities. Shipping losses were very bad, with battleships and liners and tramp steamers all suffering. The Brits were starting to reverse things, but tonnages lost were much against them.

EVACUATION OF BRITISH CHILDREN

There was much focus on the evacuation of the schoolchildren. By now, the children who had been evacuated had been away for about two weeks, and that was long enough for a bit of the euphoria to wear off. The main problems were that some children were not all that well-behaved, or clean, and that their parents were not either. Another problem was that increasing numbers of parents wanted their children back home, and this desire was growing stronger as more days passed without air-raids. Also, the mothers, who sometimes accompanied smaller children, were becoming a problem.

Some of the frictions generated are captured below.

Letters, Tom Murphy. Many mothers are feeling the pangs of separation, but cannot afford the necessary fares out of their own meagre resources, and they are naturally concerned at the prospect of being unable to see their children for an indefinite period. Excellent as was the organization for evacuation in the London area, it did not include any arrangement for reunion of parents and children and, unless mothers pay their own fares, they have to accept a situation not at all to their liking.

Reports indicate also that many children are still suffering from homesickness: they are eager to see their parents, and above all their mothers. It is pointed out that while such reunions might have an unsettling effect in some cases, they would make parents and children realize that they were within reach of one another. Stories are told of parents who can apparently afford to visit their children in motor-cars, but inquiry shows that in many instances they sacrifice more of their income than they can spare in order to satisfy themselves that their children are happy and comfortable.

Letters, M Houston. Let us face the fact that, though the evacuation scheme for schoolchildren has been fairly successful, that arranged for the mothers and babies has failed. Large numbers of them have returned to London already, and the first frost will see the return of the rest. Similarly, the first air raid will cause large numbers to rush out of London again. And it is for this contingency that provision should be made, and made with a reasonable chance of being successful.

The mothers returned to London because they could not face the altered conditions in which they found themselves, the loneliness of the country, the separation from their husbands and schoolchildren, and being obliged to live in someone else's house.

On the other hand, householders who willingly undertook to house these people under the first evacuation scheme, and who have had their houses ruined by unhouse-trained children and dirty and slovenly mothers, have stated definitely that they will not have a second batch billeted upon them, but will go to prison instead.

Letters, G Handisyde, Camelsdale Surrey. Naturally parents will desire to see their children, and *vice versa*, but in this village they already come in such numbers as to be an embarrassment to their hosts. Sometimes, they bring sandwiches with them: more often they accept refreshments from people who are very willing to be hospitable, even though their slender means are heavily taxed by trying to feed boys of 14-15 on the allowance of 8s. 6d. But it is not mainly the expense – Sunday rest and home peace is quite impossible when a crowd of 10 or 12 relations descends on a tiny cottage. This is a real problem.

One other grumble. Time and time again we hear of children in urgent need of boots or clothing, and the parents, who are already relieved of the entire cost of the children's food, will do nothing to help, refusing even to answer letters. Where the mother is now free to earn good money, whilst the family budget is relieved of the cost of several children, it does seem that the authorities should find some way of compelling them to pay in some way for the normal repairs to clothing and shoes.

Letters, Lily Boys, Women's Services, Dower House, Woodhall Spa, Lincs. We also received **dirty, ragged, verminous children (to say nothing of still dirtier mothers** with their small children), and I have been given to understand that the educational authorities disclaim any responsibility for the condition of the evacuees, as they have been on holiday for five weeks. The shelving of responsibility from one authority to another is not very helpful, and I will go further than Lady Ravensdale who infers that educational methods seem to have failed, and suggest that the public health services are to blame.

Householders in this countrified county are horrified that there are still people living in such dirty conditions and used to such dirty habits, of which they have been only too painfully made aware. It is no good having beautiful new clean schools if the unfortunate children have to return to disgusting slums.

With reference to the question of camps for mothers suggested in the letter from Miss M Burrows in the same issue, I have already strongly urged that this should be done, as the present scheme of billeting mothers and pre-school children on house-holders is quite impracticable.

Comment. The number and variety of complaints had not dropped off by the end of October. I feel certain that there is still more to come.

RECRUITING IN OZ

The Australian Government had seen a lot happen this year, and had changed its mind on matters military quite a few times. It had said that Nasho was in, and then Nasho was out. It had decided that we needed a flying squad of 10,000 elite soldiers, and then decided we did not need them. But that we might in the future. It had recruited a militia of 78,000 men, to be trained initially for a month, and this time it had gone ahead.

Now it added to the confusion by ordering that the men who **had enlisted for one month** for the militia would in fact be required to return home after that training, but return to camp **for a further three months training** soon thereafter. As you can well imagine, a number of recruits were not happy with this new contract, and wanted a way out.

Then there was further confusion because a voluntary Second AIF of 20,000 men was to be recruited. These were to be full-time soldiers, but not eligible to serve overseas. Members who had already enlisted for the militia were allowed to register a fortnight early, so as to get priority in the rush that was expected. As it turned out this month, there was no rush, though it seemed that the quota of 20,000 would be reached in time.

On top of that, as we saw last month, a very large number of people who would have enlisted were barred because of **expansion of the list of reserved occupations.** Then, another confusing factor was rates of pay, and these were in a constant state of flux. Just let me say that the military rates were well below civilian rates for men and their families, and this obviously deterred many, especially married men with children. The comments below are typical of views of the system.

Letters, A Few Militia-Men. We read in your paper that militia-men are to do four months' camp training. We as militia-men are prepared to defend our country, but why subject us to the hardship of keeping a family on 8/- a day when in our case we are taken from our work where our pay is 16/6 a day?

In some cases this will force men to give up their homes, and others who are buying houses will have to go into unnecessary debt. Surely something can be done in cases of this kind.

Letters, William Jane. I have two sons, aged 25 and 21, who **enlisted** in the military forces 12 months ago. They have been to all parades and camps, and now they are called up for a month, and for the proposed three extra months' camp. Both are public school boys with administrative positions at stake. Why not make compulsory training for **all youths**, and be fair to those who are already doing service for their country?

Letters, Medically Fit, Mornington Peninsula. As about 90 per cent of the Second AIF (20,000) will be single men, rated as privates, I think the rate of 5/- a day when New Zealand privates are to receive 7/- a day, will lead to discontent in the force. Many single men looking for jobs in the last 10 years have had to stand idle while **returned** soldiers and married men obtained preference. These men have kept going hoping for better things, only to meet with yet another bitter pill in the form of 5/- a day.

Letters, Disturbed. As was pointed out in your paper, militiamen were not aware, when they joined, that they would be required to be away for four months' training. Otherwise it is doubtful whether there would be any married men in the Militia today.

To me, as a married militiaman, it seems that we are to bear the brunt of all this upheaval while thousands of single and married men escape the losses involved.

If it were "all in", as it would be under compulsory training, then we would feel that we were all sharing the burden equally, but with the present scheme of things, the militiaman is to be penalised for his enthusiasm in joining up before being called up.

Letters, Pro Patria. The point that few married men would have joined under the conditions now proposed I consider most important. I would suggest that, in fairness, all married men should have the right to resign at the end of the month's training. They could be placed in a Militia reserve for the three years to undergo 16 days' training annually, so that their services would still be available for home defence.

Letters, K Crawleyl. Congratulations on your article showing the primary importance of the Second AIF, and the futility of the militia under present conditions. I am 22 years of age, single and physically fit, and am vitally concerned with whatever action is taken. I have no intention of joining the militia as at present constituted. I had considered joining the 20,000 force of the Second AIF, but the Minister for Defence indicated that was of only subsidiary importance in the Government's mind. When all of this is sorted out, tens of thousands of young men will come forward and answer the call. But until then, we all know it is **our** lives that might be ruined or lost, and we do not make decisions on such matters with the confused and changing information we currently are getting.

Finally on October 21st, things got a bit more confusing when the Government announced that **Nasho was back** for all 60,000 21-year-olds, effective almost immediately. It involved three months of training, jobs would be preserved while they were in camp, and a pittance would be paid, and any wives and children would starve.

Comment. It was all a mess by this time. But it should be remembered that circumstances had changed so much from the start of the year, and it could be argued that each decision made was, at the time, the right one. The fact that things were now confused just reflected the confusion in the world around. If we look for what had actually happened, we can see that there were now large numbers of men under canvas at the moment, and there was a growing capacity to recruit and train many more. Somehow, we were muddling through to the result that we might not like, but which we had to support, given the circumstances.

BRITISH CHILDREN FOR OZ?

The Lord Mayor of Melbourne came up with a bright idea. Why not, he said, have a number of British schoolchildren come to Australia, instead of going to the British countryside? He was able to muster a few arguments for his cause, and equally able to ignore the many arguments against the idea. Still, many people jumped on his bandwagon, and there was goodish support initially. Though, as we will see, it weakened as things quickly developed.

Letters, Englishman, Berwick. It seems we are lacking in initiative to allow the idea, of bringing children out here in order to escape the horrors of war, to lie dormant for want of incentive, when doubtless there are numbers of good homes in which they would receive a welcome. Now that the "Big Brother" movement has been temporarily suspended, possibly this organization might be used and a fund could be established, to which those who have the children's welfare at heart could subscribe to cover initial expenses.

If this scheme were properly organised, untold benefits might accrue, not only to the mother country, but eventually to Australia. **To escape from their present surroundings nothing could be more beneficial to children than a long sea voyage**, and parents might view it in the same light.

Letters, T Parkdale. I was much interested in the article which appeared in your columns on September 13, in which it was **suggested that British children should be brought to Australia and fed, instead of sending the food to them**. I thought that the idea would be so enthusiastically received that long ere this plans would be well advanced.

I see by the article by Mr Geoffrey Hutton on October 5 that so far there is not anything done. No doubt the Lord Mayor, at this particular time, is an exceedingly busy man, but I do hope that he, or some influential citizen, will call a meeting and let us get to work on this excellent suggestion as quickly as possible.

Letters, W Davey. The idea of bringing British children is admirable, but there is one fundamental fact which he has overlooked. **The big majority of British mothers do not like to be parted from their children.** Already we read of children who had been evacuated going back to their parents in the danger zones, and of parents going to their children. Knowing the wonderful qualities of British motherhood, I can confidently assert that the mothers of Britain will protect their young even to death, but whatever perils they have to face they will face them together.

Letters, Ken Endean. Has anyone else been keeping an eye on English newspapers? If you have, you will know that the evacuation scheme is collapsing in Britain. Mothers and children are pining for each other, and there are no air-raids to dodge. Why keep them separated? Also, many of the children arrived in the countryside dirty, poorly clothed, verminous, and uncivilised. Do we want our fair share of these? **Who is going to pay for these little blighters?** Can you tell me that parents are going to put their children onto an ocean liner to come 12,000 miles when one or two or more such ships are being torpedoed every day? This is a silly idea that should be buried at sea, and never heard of again.

Letters, W Davey. The Government has now made it impossible to put such an evacuation scheme into operation. By its decision to allow soldiers' children 9d per day, it is obvious that any funds that could have been allotted to the bringing of British children to Australia will now have to be used to maintain the children already here. There was malnutrition before; goodness knows what it will be like after children have been existing on 9d a day for a few months.

Comment. A year later, we got our first batch of these little people.

CATS AND DOGS

Letters, Jas Booth. If the proposed Malvern by-law prohibiting the keeping of dogs and cats in houses with a frontage of less than 50ft is brought forward in the interests of health and quietness, have the framers of the by-law overlooked the part these animals play in the destruction of rats and mice? Quite recently, in one of the poorer suburbs, a sleeping child was severely injured on the cheek by a rat. Does the council want ratepayers to follow the example of a Sydney grain merchant and keep snakes to deal with these vermin?

Admittedly some animals are a nuisance, but to deprive children of the fun of a pet would not only deprive them of pleasure, but would prevent their education being complete.

Letters, Siamese. To suppose that well-fed cats will not kill rats is a fallacy. My four cats are well fed, yet they have accounted for more than 100 rats. If this iniquitous by-law be put into effect, the council will be faced with a very real rat menace, detrimental to the health of the community.

Letters, Fed Up. What right have councillors to say what is to be allowed in one's home? It seems very cruel to suggest that dog lovers must part with their pets. It would be to many a bitter blow. Instead of venting their spite on poor dumb animals, councillors should look for real nuisance. I have nearly been knocked down several times by children rushing about on scooters and skates, also playing football in the streets. Should that be allowed when we have so many parks?

Also my sleep is disturbed every night, not by dogs or cats, but by the noisy milkman who runs in with the milk and then out again, banging the gate after him. When he meets another milkman he carries on a loud conversation with him. One man dumped his empty cans in front of our house every morning at 4 o'clock, and filled his bottles, until I protested. Again, I had to move out of three flats owing to loud wireless and all-night parties.

Let the councillors try to remedy such noises instead of attacking unfortunate animals who guard our houses while we sleep. The Councils are very pleased to get the dog tax.

Letters, About Time, Caulfield. I should like to express my disapproval of the prevalence of dogs in shopping areas. As a shopkeeper I can speak with feeling of their filthy habits. If we saw more of the **dog carts** our worries would be considerably lessened, and motorists who now try to avoid dogs would have fewer accidents.

Comment. By the end of October, so voluminous had been the Letters on this subject that the Editor of the *Argus* closed further correspondence.

NOVEMBER: PHONEY WAR STARTS

For Londoners, and most of the nation, the war came to a stop for the month of November. There were no air-raids, there was virtually no fighting along the Lines in France, and there were, as always, various attempts by both sides to broker a peace. At this point, people were starting to call this the "Phoney War", and **it lasted for about six months**.

Mind you, there was serious conflict going on in areas distant from London. **On the seas, Britain was losing too many ships.** The German submarines were still picking off ships of all classes, and on one weekend seven ships were sunk. It turned out that only one of these was British, and the remainder were ships of neutral nations. The German subs were also now laying mines across the shipping lanes, and these were a growing menace. So overall, British losses were still heavy. She **was** getting increasingly sophisticated in setting up convoys, and she **did** have the German fleet bottled up in harbours unable to come out. But losses at sea were constantly depressing.

Air battles were being fought daily over northern parts of Scotland and Holland and Belgium, and into Germany. It is hard to say even today what the scores were, but the Brits were holding their own. A big problem was that the Germans were developing an early form of radar that alerted them well in advance of an enemy's approach, so that many attacking bombers were being lost. Add to that, the weather was quickly closing in for Winter, and that necessarily curtailed activity. **Things were quieter here, in Oz, also.**

But Herr Hitler was not at all restful. In mid-October, he decided that **he would invade Holland, Belgium and Luxembourg on November 12.** His forces were put on alert for that date, and they were ready to go by then. **But the weather came to the rescue.** Hitler reckoned that he needed a period of five consecutive clear days in order to make a successful attack, and anyone knowing that area of Europe will tell you how unlikely that was at that time of year. He was forced to delay the advances for months, and by then his aggression took another approach.

Apart from the slowness of the War, Britain had good news from another source in November. **America repealed its Neutrality Act.** That meant that she could now **legally** supply all sorts of weapons and munitions to the belligerents in the European sphere. England had had the foresight to place large orders for these early in the War, so she was first cab off the rank, and within days, hundreds of planes were aboard freighters destined for England.

Germany would have been legally entitled to buy the same goods, but such was American public distaste for all things German that she was not openly able to get much at all. Besides, at about the same time, the US started to extended credit to Britain, but did not extend it to the Germans. So this latter nation got to actually pay **now** for the goods, whereas Britain got them on the never-never. This meant that Germany virtually missed out on this tremendous source of war materials.

Within Britain, a threatening failure of one of Britain's great institutions was scary.

Press report. When the War broke out, English pubs suddenly displayed disheartening notices that in the event of an air raid warning, customers "must get out and make their own arrangements." The pubs, which had remained unchanging centres of traditional hospitality, sociability, and mutual commiseration through changing eras of happiness, stress, perplexity and danger, lost their ancient and venerable status.

Now, however, the Minister for Home Security, Sir John Anderson, sensing the bitter disappointment in the hearts of hundreds of thousands of Englishmen, recommends that **the owners of pubs should make their cellars and other accommodation available in the event of raids.**

"If the owners adopt the recommendation, it will be generally agreed that Britain is back on track, and ready for practically anything."

Comment. As you can gather, the situation, though serious, did not get out of hand, and you will be pleased to know that there is still the odd pub or two scattered round the grand nation.

EVACUATION OF CHILDREN

More British Letters and social comment abounded. It got harder every day, without air raids, to convince people that a country sojourn was necessary. This good analysis below summarises the thoughts of many.

Letters, Juvenile Welfare Officer, Warwick. The groups we received numbered 1,107 children. Of these, **only 224 remained in the reception areas** at the time of this inquiry, and, of the 224, 150 were determined to return home as soon as they reached the school-leaving age. Thus only seven per cent were willing to remain in a reception area. These figures are first hand and authentic. Such indications force one to the conclusion that the evacuation system cannot under present conditions survive the Christmas holiday, if it lasts till then.

The inquiry has suggested three principal reasons for the breakdown.

First, the failure to provide school camps before evacuation took place, to which **schools could have been moved as undisturbed units**, so preserving the normal abundant parental confidence in teachers and school institutions. Billeting has proved a substitute effective only in the direst emergency. The excessive secrecy as to destinations which was imposed on every one also prevented the building up beforehand of parental confidence: there was too much mystery about the whole business. School camps, known and approved of, would have evoked a very different parental attitude.

Secondly, the decision to call for parental financial contributions should have been made at the outset, without ambiguity, instead of at a time when cracks were already appearing in the structure. It is only **now** that parents are finding out that they are up for six shillings a week for each child for upkeep. If that had been known earlier, lots of children would not have gone in the first place. This is causing widespread resentment.

The third cause is the uncompromisingly negative attitude adopted towards those children who have remained in city areas, sometimes for quite understandable reasons (such as possession at home of Anderson shelters or strong cellars).

Parents were told that evacuation was quite voluntary, but now those who did not send their children are officially regarded as fools and blind. Council schools, often the soundest buildings in the district, remain closed, while private schools and "business colleges," run as profit-making concerns, remain unrestrictedly and ostentatiously open. This again has aroused much needless prejudice against evacuation.

I do not write this letter in favour of abandonment of evacuation; it is merely a description of things as they are.

The youths mentioned here were within eight months of leaving elementary school. But a similar, though not so pronounced, trend was occurring at other ages. More and more children were leaving the country and going back to the city. The news report below described the dilemma that the Government was in.

HOUSE OF LORDS: RE-OPEN SCHOOLS?

News`item. The problems of evacuation, and especially those of the education of children whose parents have brought them back to city areas, were reviewed in the House of Lords tonight.

Lord De La Warr pointed out that the Government had to face the task caused by the presence in city areas of more than half the school children who could be at school in safe country areas, but were now receiving little or no education. That situation could not be allowed to exist, but the Government was unwilling to make evacuation compulsory in any but the most desperate circumstances, and it was driven to some measure of reopening of schools in city areas. But his advice to parents was to leave their children in the safer places.

The Government had decided that such schools as were available in city areas should be reopened for children whose parents wished them to attend. It might be necessary in many cases to adopt **the double-shift system**, under which children would attend for only part of the day. Some protection against air raids would be provided, but if serious raids should occur the schools would be closed.

Comment.   The evacuation scheme was falling apart. If bombing attacks did occur, probably many children who had returned home to the cities would want to return to the country. **And probably many homes in the country would not want those children back.**

On the other hand, if no raids occurred, even more children would go home. But all sorts of adults had moved to the country to care for them. At what point would they be repatriated? And would that process be reversed if air-raids then did occur? A multitude of such questions was arising, and every day there were no answers, only more questions.

SOME QUICK BRITISH FACTS

Italy had not joined the War as yet. Mussolini and Ciano had one foot firmly planted in Hitler's camp, but were really trying hard to broker a peace.

The new Japanese Cabinet was not nearly so jingoistic as the old one. Now it had agreed to stop harassing British interests in China and stop the anti-British demonstrations in Tokyo.

The Brits from next month would have **one hour less of blackout every evening**, and one hour less at the dawn.

Theatres and sporting events were back on the calender.

ENLISTMENTS IN OZ

Enlistment for the Second AIF was proceeding fairly well. The great rush that some people expected had not eventuated, but numbers **were** fairly close to targets. **The Air force, however, had been given a big fillip.** Britain had decided that she was desperately short of fighter pilots and other air crew, and that she could get some of these from the Empire. So she liaised with Australia, Canada and India, in particular, to set up an **Empire Training Scheme**, whereby young men would be recruited and quickly taught to fly and fight, and enter the RAF in England. **The most glamorous job in the whole war scene** was that of fighter pilot, so young men across that nation were now eagerly awaiting more details of the fast-evolving scheme.

CANTEENS: WET OR DRY?

Military training was now going ahead quite well, both for the militia and for the Second AIF. About 10,000 men were entering camps every month. But a controversy grew over whether alcohol should be made available for sale in their military canteens.

For those of you who have not been lucky enough to serve time in the Oz armed forces, let me point out that at the end of a normal training day, troops go to the mess and have what is often called a meal. After that, sometimes they get a night off, and are free to go to a canteen and buy small items. In 1939, the best seller would have been smokes. Also, another seller would have been beer, if it had been for sale, even allowing for the tender years of some of the new soldiers.

The question now became whether beer should be on sale at these canteens. One argument against wet canteens came from Temperance Societies and church groups, such as the Methodists and Presbyterians, who argued that consumption of alcohol was morally wrong, and was especially so for young men. Their arguments were often supported by quotes from the Bible, and also requests to be allowed to set up facilities for selling fruit juices and milk shakes at the canteens. They were supported by a host of mums, and dads, who saw wet canteens as a danger for their sons. A few people objected on the grounds that alcoholic hangover would impair their performance the next day, and also on the grounds that long term drinking had very serious effects.

Some supporters of wet canteens argued that alcohol was legally served elsewhere, and should be served in the army. Others said that arguments against alcohol usually assumed that it would be drunk to excess, and there was no reason for this, especially if the pig-swill conditions prevailing elsewhere were replaced by a sensible environment.

Another argument was that for the militia, who were quite young, dry canteens would be acceptable. The Second AIF, however, were definitely older, and were enlisted for a long term, and might be called on to serve overseas. So surely they should be treated as adults, and provided with wet canteens. After all, the Officers had them.

A sample of other arguments is given below.

Letters, F Puaux, Consul de France, Melbourne. I cannot pass without a protest the letter of Mr Ambrose Roberts published in your paper, concerning the pretended effects of wine-drinking on the health and physical condition of the French troops around the world.

It is not for me to seek motives or to take sides in the discussion concerning "wine in camps" in Australia. But as a Frenchman, and one who drinks wine, may I point out to your correspondent that he makes numerous errors. It is the common practice in France, in every class of society, to drink wine with meals. The great majority of medical men favour this custom. Workmen, particularly in the country, would refuse to work if their employers refused them a certain number of litres of wine a day. The "quart" of wine has become a tradition in the French Army, and the reward of the French soldier, on great occasions, is an increase of his wine rations.

"Honest" wine with a moderate alcoholic content is a good, healthy drink. Refreshing and strengthening, wine helps the soldier to bear the fatigue of military duties.

Mr Ambrose Roberts in his too great enthusiasm for his crusade has, I fear, condemned wine in ignorance of its virtue. The restraint which my functions impose upon me cannot prevent me from saying that the magnificent Australian soldiers could only benefit by a moderate consumption.

The drinking of wine to excess when fasting leads to alcoholic ills. That is undisputed. But to deduce from this that wine should be prohibited is a manifest exaggeration. In all things we should avoid extremes.

Letters, Matron, Newcastle. The scenes on the trains and on the platforms from Sydney to Ingleburn yesterday afternoon would convert any sane person to the necessity for wet canteens in the camps – and also some restriction on the unlimited sale of bottled beer to young men in uniform.

I had to move from the carriage in the train I was travelling in. It was a pitiful sight to see lads of 18 or so staggering all over the place, their pockets and arms filled with beer bottles to take back to camp. **I am sure a wet canteen under supervision, and restriction on the sale of bottled beer from hotels, is the correct solution.**

Letters, DRINKER, Ashfield. As a recruit for the Second AIF, I can point out that there is no way that anyone can stop the drinkers here from getting and drinking grog. Already in the towns round the camps we have sly-grog shops setting up, and bootleg suppliers smuggling grog into camp. **Any one who wants a beer can get one.** Every night our Company gets a large number of bottles delivered to various points on the edge of camp, and our official sentries mind this lot until morning comes and we can come and get it. This does not mean we get drunk every day. It just means we can sit at the end of a hard day, and have a quiet beer with our mates.

Maybe your wowser letter–writers would be better people if they did the same.

SOME THOUGHTS ON MENTAL HEALTH

In every State in Australia, the provision of what we now call Mental Health services was in a state of infancy in 1939. Below is a Letter that talks about some small aspects of the problem. It concerns the distinction between **the mentally deficient on the one hand, and the criminally insane on the other**. When you think about it, the two groups are very different indeed. But then, and to some extent even now, the two groups were lumped together, and you might even say they were put into the one "too hard" basket.

Letters, K Cunningham, Director, Australian Council for Educational Research. To place the care of **mental defectives** in the hands of the Department charged with the care of **the insane**, as is proposed, would be a mistake. In my opinion the chief weakness of the bill is its failure to provide proper machinery for the examination and certification of defectives. One notices with concern that any medical practitioner's certificate is apparently sufficient to commit a child to an institution for at least a month. **The vast majority of medical practitioners are not competent to apply the forms of examination essential for the proper certification of mental deficiency.** Even the psychiatrist as such does not normally cover this in his course of training. Most feeble-minded individuals are not suffering from mental disorder, but from a lack of innate intellectual capacity, and the problem of assessing this is fundamentally an educational and psychological one.

Personal comment. As I have written this series of books, I have watched the States chop and change their approach to "mental health" in its many different forms. It has always been the poor cousin of Health proper and has never attracted the serious attention and finance that such a big problem deserves.

NATIONAL SERVICE FOR PIGEONS

Press report. A register of carrier pigeons for use in wartime is being compiled by the Air Ministry. The pigeons would be carried in RAF machines and used to convey messages if an aeroplane's wireless apparatus were put out of action. With the outbreak of War, the RAF has created a pigeon service, and at Calshot and two centres overseas it breeds and trains carrier pigeons of its own.

During the crisis last September the Air Ministry received offers of pigeons from thousands of fanciers. All the offers were filed, and on this basis a national register is being prepared. Owners of pigeons seem keen to place them at the Government's disposal, and it is expected that about 500,000 of the birds will be available to play a part in national defence. That part might well be vitally important. With a moderate tail wind, a good bird will fly at 1,600 yards a minute over 300 miles, and in highly favourable conditions speeds of over a mile a minute have been reached. The highest speed claimed for a carrier pigeon is a mile and a half a minute over 300 miles.

TOP MOVIES OF 1939

Huckleberry Finn	Mickey Rooney
Sherlock Holmes	Basil Rathbone
Thin Man	William Powell
Andy Hardy	Mickey Rooney
At the Circus	Marx Brothers
Bachelor Mother	Ginger Rodgers
Beau Geste	Gary Cooper
Cat and the Canary	Bob Hope
Confessions of a Nazi Spy	Edward G Robinson
Drums among the Mohawk	Henry Fonda
Goodbye Mr Chips	Robert Donut
Gone with the Wind	Vivien and Clark
Wurthering Heights	Laurence Olivier
Babes in Arms	Mickey Rooney
Mr Smith goes to Washington	James Stewart

TOP SONGS OF 1939

Over the Rainbow	Judy Garland
Moonlight Sonata	Glenn Miller
God Bless America	Kate Smith
Saints go Marching in	Louis Armstrong
Deep Purple	Bing Crosby
Auld Lang Syne	Guy Lombardo
I Wonder who's Kissing her now	Bing Crosby
Little Brown Jug	Glenn Miller
Jeepers Creepers	Louis Armstrong
South of the Border	Shep Fields
Tea for Two	Art Tatum
Scatter-Brain	Frankie Masters
If I didn't Care	The Ink Spots

Challenge. I picked these songs out of a longer list because I can remember them and their artists. Can you?

DECEMBER: FOREIGN DOCTORS

Letters, A Robson. It is most perplexing and alarming that the State Cabinet should go back on the former decision of the House, in spite of a strong public opinion favouring the appointment of German refugee doctors to the remote districts of New South Wales.

Those of us who have had the pleasure of knowing some of these doctors personally realise what benefits the Cabinet and the British Medical Association are withholding from the community. Moreover, the public-at-large also knows this, as evidenced by its strong support for the appointment of refugee doctors. Our sense of fair play demands that we should give these men who have come as doctors into our midst a fair chance to use the knowledge and skill which they have gained abroad. These new Australians can be a blessing to many a person in the State, if only we will give them a chance.

Letters, One Viewpoint. By what special right does the medical world claim to close its doors to refugees? Among other sections of the community – musicians, many skilled employments, and shopkeepers, and so on – the attitude towards migrants is more sympathetic and friendly, although it is not to be supposed that competition in these spheres means less than to a doctor. The Medical Association has a duty to make sure that a newcomer possesses the necessary qualifications to practise, but when it refuses to allow any would-be Australians to join its ranks and share some of the material benefits of medical practice, it lays itself open to the charge of acting suspiciously like the harshest forms of business combines or monopolies.

Comment. The British Medical Association was then the Trade Union for doctors in Australia.

Second comment. The persecution of aliens and refugees in Australia would get a lot worse next year.

FINLAND FIGHTS BACK

Throughout November, Russia had been pushing Finland into granting it rights to ports and other facilities, and asking to set up military bases in the land. Finland, though worried by these not-so-friendly approaches, had not rolled over like the other Baltic States had, and it had said "no" when it thought it proper.

Early in the month of December, it paid the price for this brave display of defiance. The armed forces of Russia bombed the capital, Stockholm, and shelled various ports round the seafront, and made a military advance with a million men, crossing the border in dozens of places along its entire length.

For a week, it looked as if Russia would have a complete walk-over. It had the tanks and planes and manpower that Finland did not have. **But then winter came to Finland's rescue.** It turned out there was a large area that was swampland and rivers not yet frozen over, and so the Red Army tanks were severely restricted in where they could go. Then, the ghastly weather kept planes grounded most of the time. As well, in their white fur-lined warm uniforms, the Finnish troops were trained to move sleekly about on skis, while the poor Russians were plodding though the snow in big clod-hoppers. In the very long nights of the Finnish winter, these advantages played into the hands of the will-o-the-wisp Finn forces.

So, the Russian advance was slowed. By the end of the month, **the Finns had even moved onto Soviet soil at some points**. But then it was time for a winter break, and both Armies were forced to dig in, with Finland for the moment well pleased with itself for having stood up to Europe's newest bully.

Comment. There is a sad ending to this story, in the New Year. For the next two months, until the snow thawed, the Russians thought about all the mistakes they had made in their first offensive, and conjured up ways to do things better. When fighting resumed, they again invaded with considerable ease, and in a matter of weeks, Russia had conquered the small nation. In March 1940, they were able to impose settlement terms on the Finns much harsher than their original demands, so one more bit of Europe fell to blatant aggression.

Second comment. If you look again at a map of Europe, you can see how Europe was being carved up. Perhaps you might like to get out your crayons, and mark in the changes. You could mark in Austria, the Czechs and two-thirds of Poland, to the Germans. Then one third of Poland, and all of Latvia, Lithuania and Estonia, to the Russians. And finally, add Finland also to the Red collection. It looks depressing, and while I cannot anticipate history, I have the feeling that things might get even worse next year.

Third comment. The numbers killed are staggering. Statistics in war-time are always lies. But eighty years later, they are usually fairly reliable. Current estimates are that the Russians lost at least 50,000 men in this campaign. I can tell you that I cannot begin to think about this, and I cannot put the horror of it into words. I have to leave you by yourself to contemplate it. But, I must sadly add, **there was worse to come.**

THE *GRAF SPEE*

The German pocket battleship *Graf Spee* had put to sea before the declaration of war, and so was quite well positioned in the Southern Atlantic to destroy merchant vessels coming out of South American ports, and headed for Britain. Over the last two months, she had been marauding with enough success to attract the Royal Navy's special interest, so much so that a special hunting pack of three destroyers were given the task of putting her out of action.

On December 13, this pack made contact with the enemy, and after a naval battle at some horizon-distance, forced the damaged *Graf Spee* to retreat, and head to Uruguay's capital, Montevideo, for repairs. Two of the three British destroyers loitered outside the port, and were joined by many other Royal Navy vessels. The *Graf Spee* found that the damage to herself was fairly severe, and there was difficulty in getting the local labour force to work on her repairs. By international law for belligerents, she would have to leave the estuary within three days. Her Commander pointed out to Hitler that she was in no condition to fight a running battle against the forces massed against it on the open sea. Hitler ordered that the ship be scuttled near the mouth of the harbour.

Thus, after three days, this course of action was followed. Her crew were evacuated by lighter, and as was the tradition, the Captain was the last to leave. The Captain saw to his duties for another 24 hours, and **then committed suicide.** The waiting British ships were robbed of a victory at sea, but at home the news was received with enormous glee. "The first sea battle of the War" had been won by the British. Churchill said in Parliament that "The effects of the action off the River Plate gave intense joy to the British people and enhanced our prestige throughout the world." It truly was a great Christmas present for Britain and the whole British Empire.

Letter from Sydney, A Herborn, Mosman. It is reported that Winston Churchill, "**scornfully** referred to the *Graf Spee's* disregard of the honourable course of fighting to the death."

Apparently it has not occurred to the First Lord that the action of the Captain of this vessel not only saved the lives of his own crew, but also of many British seamen who would inevitably been killed had a further battle taken place. **Cannot we get rid of the idea that honour is only gained by killing as many men as possible?**

BRITISH NEWS IN BRIEF

Hitler had promised that **he would not bomb Britain's cities**. So far, he had kept his promise, and all the sandbags and black-outs and air-raid shelters had been of no use.

Thus more and more **school children** were coming home from the country, and the numbers were growing as Christmas got close. Many more city schools were re-opening their doors, and the authorities were dithering.

The Army in France had hibernated with no action at all. The Royal Navy was still active, and so too was the Air Force. But in the latter case, there were no definitive battles, and the activities were still restricted to Scottish ports and the Channel and coastal land adjacent.

Sugar and meat were to be added to the goods on rationing from next month, joining bacon and butter.

With a great deal of fanfare and ballyhoo, the movie "**Gone with the Wind**" opened in London.

The number of wardens and other ARP workers in Britain was officially quoted as over 700,000 at the end of the year.

The first airmen from Australia arrived in England on December 27th, and were given a "rapturous welcome."

OTHER BRITISH LETTERS

Letters, W Cocks. No one can fail to appreciate the efforts that are being made for the recognition, comfort and welfare of the soldiers of the various departments of His Majesty's forces on land, in the air, and in the Navy. I have looked in vain for any similar efforts being made for the men of **the Merchant Navy**.

The men who man these vessels keep England supplied with foodstuffs from overseas, that carry our exports and imports, armaments and ammunition in the face of many and grave dangers. Their calling prevents their enjoying much of home life or home comforts. No brass band or procession marks their coming or going. They wear no uniform, but they are "doing their bit" in helping to win the war equally with other branches of the service. I do trust they will not be overlooked in the distribution of the comforts which are being so generously provided by the many organizations interested in the men who are serving their King and country.

OZ MILITARY MATTERS

Pay rates for our militia were raised from five shillings per day to eight. At the same time however, it was announced **that the militia would be disbanded from next June**, so volunteer training would be a thing of the past.

The Second AIF would then become our major military force, even though it involved long-term service, and also the possibility of service overseas. To encourage this, the Canberra brains **cut** the rate of pay for this force from six shillings to five shillings, but did increase deferred pay (for when they left the Army in several years) from one shilling to two per day.

Comment. A pay cut is not the normal the way to encourage applicants to a job. But patriotic feeling in the nation was rising, and recruitment to the Second AIF was more or less on target. So it seemed reasonable to gamble for a few months on getting the numbers needed

Second comment. After a lot of chopping and changing, under enormously uncertain conditions, this nation was finally on the path to putting its army on the right footing. Though the next Letter, concerning the numbers involved, puts some perspective on this.

Letters, Australian Native, Balwyn. The bulk of the Second AIF have only been in camp about one month, and I am at a loss to understand the violent hurry to embark in a few weeks' time a force without sufficient training, guns, and equipment. Some of the men are very young, and many of the men, when they enlisted, understood they were to be Australia's first line of defence, but to go abroad, if necessary. It was then common knowledge that France had 5,000,000 trained soldiers and Great Britain had only called up portion of her land forces. At this stage, the almost immediate embarkation of our men appears to be somewhat theatrical and probably ill-advised. Why not train them thoroughly in Australia before departure?

PROPAGANDA AGAIN

The newspapers were full of goody-goody feature stories of how good military life was. **It appears** the recruits spent an inordinate amount of time at concerts, and the performing artists were always the best in the world, though strangely unknown until now. Mateship seemed to abound, scuffles and fights between rivals were not heard of, pilfering and unlawful absences did not appear in this model Army, and "the lads", though happy to go home for leave, were always even more happy to return to camp. In fact, some were "so anxious to get back that they often returned a half-day early."

There were a few people, deviants no doubt, who saw things a bit differently.

Letters, Wellwisher. Your leading article "The Cinderella Force" was timely. When I went to visit my son at Seymour a week ago he had with him a few of his tent mates. While they were enjoying the life, and very keen, they were definitely critical about the scarcity of food, and its poor quality. They told me that on three different occasions that week, flies had got to it. My son has been in camp about a month. It cost me 6 Pounds 1 Shilling to provide him with an outfit, and it is only within the last day or so that he has been issued with overalls and a few other items. As I have had over 40 years in the boot trade I took an interest in their boots, and I consider that five or six weeks would be their limit in wet weather.

Letters, Ex-Officer. Young friends of mine are ashamed to appear outside camp in the badly-fitting uniforms supplied to them, and it is not in the least surprising. I have served with the Army in different parts of the world, and have never seen troops so badly dressed as are the AIF. It is to be hoped that they will be properly clothed before leaving for overseas, and not sent abroad in the comic state in which they appear in Sydney. It should be remembered that they will be closely associated with the British Army, whose troops are amongst the best dressed in the world.

Letters, J Shepherd. It is announced that when the Australians arrive at their destination overseas, they will be fitted out in the same uniform as worn by the Royal Air Force, with a badge, only, to distinguish them as Australians. Although every branch of the Allied war service is fighting as one unit, and for the one common objective, let the Australian airman retain his Australian uniform, as do the Infantry and the Light Horse, etc. The seed of a great tradition was sown by the Australian soldier and airman in the Great War.

England has been bathing in traditional glory for over 10 centuries – Australia for a quarter of a century – and our hope is that the lads who go overseas will be permitted to retain their identity in the nature of a uniform that has already won fame for this young country in the air.

TALKING AT BRIDGE

Letters, FED-UP. Have you ever been to a charity bridge party? How anyone can play bridge under the conditions that exist at most of these charity bridge parties is beyond me. As soon as the women enter the room, it seems to be a signal for them to start talking, and the din and chatter continues right throughout the afternoon until, at the end of the time, one leaves, thoroughly exhausted, and vowing never to go gain.

Why not suggest to the organisers of these charity bridge parties that all chatter must cease during play. Let them talk before the play begins, and during the teatime, but try and preserve some degree of quietness during play.

SUMMING UP 1939

Then versus now. To review 1939, I look back to January, and note how things have changed. In both Australia and Britain, the emphasis on military matters has grown to an enormous extent. At the beginning of the year, it was easy to pluck a few Trivia items from the newspapers, but at the end of the year, I need to seek them more rigorously. Trivia in society has given way to trivia about the War, and the papers are full of it.

It is noticeable how much blatant propaganda is printed. This is the type of stuff that says in a sortie over the English Channel, twelve German aircraft were shot down and only two of ours were damaged. Day after day such stories were issued by the Propaganda Departments, and duly printed. Then there were reports of expected revolts in Germany, that the German people in the Saar were starving, and that in Poland nuns had been used as clappers in the bells of Danzig. Poison gas is being used by the Nazis in Finland. **Most of the stories were simply unbelievable**, and became the subject of ridicule,especially in the London *Times*.

Advertisements were often now cast in military terms. Public discussion on radio, newsreels in theatres, and opinions of the man-in-the-street were all concentrated on the War. There was a growing amount of talk that young men must join up to the military, and that those who did not were shirking their duty. The new soldier recruits coming home on leave were treated as heroes, and girls who previously would not look at them now were in the scramble to be seen with them. It wasn't just **the soldier**. Air Force men were in special demand, and it turned out – if you believe the young men themselves – that almost every one of these was a pilot. And of course, all the nice girls loved a sailor.

But even at the end of the year, Australians had no concept of what was ahead of them. Britain was a long way away, and anyway that War over there was turning out to be a Phoney War. Not only that, the Japanese had stopped harassing the British, and so there was nothing to worry about there. But, the worry **did** persist.

Most people could see war coming into their lives**, but had no concept of it actually coming to our shores.** It all seemed too far away for the majority. **But there were some who were truly worried. The families, of those airmen who had just arrived in England, realised all of a sudden that their sons would possibly be killed.** Likewise for the Second AIF who might be shipped out and into France at any time. These were people who would soon be looking at the newspapers every day, and every day dreading *the postman* bringing those neat little letters and telegrams **announcing the death of their kin.** But overall, the mood in Australia was hopeful and watchful.

On that note, I will close this book. I am happy to report that 1939 was **not** as dreadful a year as you might have expected, in terms of the War. I suppose that, after that, if everything had gone on for another year at the same pace, everyone would still have been worried, but would have felt a bit relieved. **But that did not happen.** The situation deteriorated badly next year.

When I have closed **other books** in this Series, those that covered the post-War years, I have ended on a high note, with a summary that said things had been pretty good this year, and would be better next. I think that I was right in every case. **But this is not true for 1939. Sad to say,** this year was not so good, and no matter how you looked at it, next year would prove to be **a lot** worse.

READERS' COMMENTS

Tom Lynch, Speers Point. Some history writers make the mistake of trying to boost their authority by including graphs and charts all over the place. You on the other hand get a much better effect by saying things like "he made a pile". Or "every one worked hours longer than they should have, and felt like death warmed up at the end of the shift." I have seen other writers waste two pages of statistics painting the same picture as you did in a few words.

Barry Marr, Adelaide You know that I am being facetious when I say that I wish the war had gone on for years longer so that you would have written more books about it.

Edna College, Auburn. A few times I stopped and sobbed as you brought memories of the postman delivering letters, and the dread that ordinary people felt as he neared. How you captured those feelings yet kept your coverage from becoming maudlin or bogged down is a wonder to me.

Betty Kelly, Wagga Wagga. Every time you seem to be getting serious, you throw in a phrase or memory that lightens up the mood. In particular, in the war when you were describing the terrible carnage of Russian troops, you ended with a ten-line description of how aggrieved you felt and ended it with "apart from that, things are pretty good here". For me, it turned the unbearable into the bearable, and I went from feeling morbid and angry back to a normal human being.

Alan Davey, Brisbane. I particularly liked the light-hearted way you described the scenes at the airports as American, and British, high-flying entertainers flew in. I had always seen the crowd behaviour as disgraceful, but your light-hearted description of it made me realise it was in fact harmless and just good fun.

In 1964, HMAS Voyager, an Australian destroyer, was sunk in a collision with the air-craft carrier, Melbourne. Stamp collecting was disappearing as a hobby, wine was no longer plonk, and mothers were waging war on old-fashioned tuck-shops. (God bless them. The tuck-shops, not the mothers). The Beatle cult was angering some people. The Tab: to be on not to be? Can true Reds get fat? Did Billie Graham have lasting effects? Prostitution was proposed as a safety valve against rape. Judy Garland got bad Press in Melbourne and left Oz in a sulk.

In 1967, postcodes were introduced, and you could pay your debts with a new five-dollar note. You could talk-back on radio, about a brand new ABS show called "This Day Tonight." Getting a job was easy with unemployment at 1.8 % – better that the 5% 50 years later. Arthur Calwell left at last. Whitlam took his place. Harold Holt drowned, and Menzies wrote his first book in retirement.

****

THERE ARE 33 TITLES IN THIS SERIES

For questions and orders and deliveries, contact Jennie on 0438 732519, or at jen@boombooks.biz

In 1968, Sydney had its teeth fluoridated, its sobriety tested for alcohol with breathalisers, and its first Kentucky Fried. And it first heart transplant. There was still much opposition to the Vietnam War and demos, often violent, were everywhere all the time. The casino in Tasmania was approved. We won a pot of gold at the Olympics, Lionel Rose became the first Aboriginal to become a World Boxing Champion, and poet Dorothea Mackellar died at the age of 82.

In 1970, President Nixon's war in Vietnam, and now Cambodia, was getting unpopular in the USA and

Oz. Melbourne's Westgate Bridge fell into the water and killed 35 workmen. The Queen, Prince Phillip, and two kids came to Oz. They liked it, so the Pope came later. Margaret Court, John Newcombe, Shane Gould, and Raylene Boyle all did well overseas, and made us think we were world-beaters. Nick Jagger starred in "Ned Kelly".

****

Chrissi and birthday books for Mum and Dad and Aunt and Uncle and cousins and family and friends and work and everyone else.
Don't forget a good read and chuckle for yourself.

These books, soft cover and hard cover, are available
from the one-stop shop at boombooks.biz

Soft covers for each of the years from 1939 to 1971

Hard covers from 1939 and 1940
Hard covers from 1949 and 1950
Hard covers from 1958 and 1960
Hard covers from 1969 and 1970

Express Post also available

WEB SITE AT www.boombooks.biz HAS ALL THE
DESCRIPTIONS AND DETAILS YOU NEED